MW01154961

THE LIBRARY OF
THE VILLA DEI PAPIRI
at Herculaneum

DAVID SIDER

THE LIBRARY OF
THE VILLA DEI PAPIRI
at Herculaneum

Los Angeles, The J. Paul Getty Museum

© 2005 J. Paul Getty Trust

Getty Publications
1200 Getty Center Drive, Suite 500
Los Angeles, California 90049-1682
www.getty.edu

Christopher Hudson, *Publisher*
Mark Greenberg, *Editor in Chief*

Benedicte Gilman, *Manuscript Editor*
David Mellen, *Designer*
Stacy Miyagawa, *Production Coordinator*
David Fuller, *Cartographer*
Marian Stewart, *Draftswoman*
Carol Roberts, *Indexer*

Printed in China by Imago

Frontispiece: Papyrus plants (*Cyperus papyrus*), as pictured
in the frontispiece of John Hayter, *A Report upon the
Herculaneum Manuscripts in a Second Letter, addressed, by
permission, to his royal highness the Prince Regent* (London,
1811). Los Angeles, Research Library, Getty Research Institute.
See p. 54, for Hayter's activities in Naples.

Unless otherwise noted, all illustrations are reproduced by
permission of the owners.

Library of Congress Cataloging-in-Publication Data

Sider, David
    The library of the Villa dei Papiri at Herculaneum/
David Sider
    p. cm.
Includes bibliographical references and index.
ISBN-13: 978-0-89236-799-3 (pbk.)
ISBN-10: 0-89236-799-7 (pbk.)
1. Villa of the Papyri (Herculaneum) 2. Herculaneum
(Extinct city)—Antiquities. 3. Piso Caesoninus, Lucius
Calpurnius—Library. 4. Private libraries—Italy—
Herculaneum (Extinct city) 5. Manuscripts, Greek
(Papyri)—Italy—Herculaneum (Extinct city) I. Title.
    DG70.H5S565 2005
    091'.0937'7—dc22
                                        2004028792

CONTENTS

Preface and Acknowledgments

This work draws freely on the scholarship of others, not all of whom are identified in the notes and bibliography, where books and articles in English are favored. Since, however, it is impossible to proceed beyond an elementary level in the study of Herculaneum and Epicureanism without Italian (and to suggest otherwise by failing to note this would be seriously misleading), I refer readers to the most important of these contributions. Unless otherwise stated, all translations are my own. Greek names for the most part have not been transliterated as the Romans did, but in a way that more closely accords with the original Greek alphabet; thus, Bakkhylides rather than Bacchylides and Herakleitos rather than Heraclitus. Nonetheless, some familiar Latinate forms remain, most notably Herculaneum rather than Herakleion and Aristotle rather than Aristoteles. And Epikouros's followers are Epicureans.

Care must also be taken to recognize which system of transliteration is being used, as I quote and cite authors who employ the Latinate system or refer to ancient authors in other modern languages. Note in particular the problems caused by names that end in -o and -on. Thus (Greek) Ariston becomes Aristo in Latin, which is to be distinguished from (Greek) Aristos, a man's name, or (Greek) Aristo, which is a woman's name (cf. Sappho). This problem began as soon as Latin took over Greek names; for example, the Latin poet Catullus refers to someone, who may be Philodemos, as Socration, but this name in its Latin form may represent either of two Greek names, Sokratiōn, a name in its own right, or (as I think) Sokratiŏn ("little Sokrates"), the latter of which ends in the diminutive -ion, which, to confuse things still further, can be a male or female nickname, such as Leontion, the learned woman who was Epikouros's fellow philosopher and bedmate. (All the names in -ion in Philodemos's epigrams are women.) And watch out for Italian, whose Aristo represents Greek Aristos, whereas (Italian) Aristone = (Greek) Ariston = (Latin) Aristo.

In writing this book, I have enjoyed the scholarly kindness of friends who have spent many hours over many years working with the Herculaneum papyri and with the archives that hold their fascinating history. Francesca Longo Auricchio, Giuliana Leone, and Giovanni Indelli in Naples offered valuable advice about the widely dispersed literature on the subject I was to write about. Dr. Leone guided my wife and me through the Officina dei Papiri in Naples, where most of the papyri are now housed, and where we were given permission to take photographs. From Valerio Papaccio, an architect working for the Soprintendenza of Herculaneum and Pompeii, I learned about the current and possible future state of the excavations of the Villa dei Papiri. Dirk Obbink instructed me in the drawings made of the papyri now in Oxford and he and Nikolaos Gonis made it easy for me to photograph papyri belonging to the Egyptian Exploration Society. The multispectral images are thanks to Roger Macfarlane. I am also grateful to Patricia Kane of the Fordham University Rare Book Room for facilitating the photographing of an item in that collection. David Blank read and offered comments on the chapters dealing with the history of the papyri and their unrolling; Richard Janko read those on the contents of the papyri; and Francesca Longo Auricchio then read the entire manuscript. The translations of archival material by David Blank are used with his kind permission. To all, I am extremely grateful; and to all I offer my apologies for where I failed to learn from them. Please do not hold them responsible for any flaws that remain. At the Getty, I am grateful to Mary Louise Hart for first inviting me to write about the Villa's library, and to Benedicte Gilman and Kenneth Lapatin for their editorial support from beginning to end of this very pleasurable project. I am also grateful to my wife Sandra for her contributions.

ABBREVIATIONS

bibl.	bibliography
ca.	circa
cm	centimeter
col./cols.	[text] column/columns
CErc	*Cronache Ercolanesi*
cf.	compare
ch.	chapter
col.	column
ed.	editor/edited by
edn.	edition
esp.	especially
f./ff.	following
fr./frr.	fragment/fragments
ft.	foot/feet
Gr.	Greek
H.	height
HV	*Herculanensium Voluminum quae supersunt*
in.	inch
Ital.	Italian
km	kilometer
L.	Latin
max. dim.	maximum dimension
m	meter
ms./mss.	manuscript/manuscripts
n./nn.	note/notes
p./pp.	page/pages
PHerc.	*Papyrus Herculanensis*
r.	ruled/ruler
repr.	reprint
sc.	scilicet (that is)
suppl.	supplement
trans.	translation/translator/translated by
yd.	yard
ZPE	*Zeitschrift für Papyrologie und Epigraphik*

MAP OF THE BAY OF NAPLES REGION

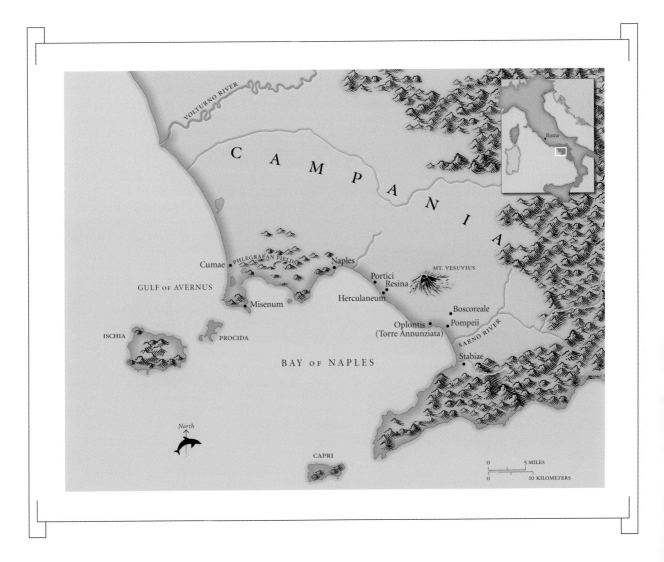

VOLTURNO RIVER

C A M P A N I A

Rome

Cumae
PHLEGRAEAN FIELDS
Naples

GULF OF AVERNUS
Portici
Resina
MT. VESUVIUS

Misenum
Herculaneum

Boscoreale

ISCHIA
Oplontis
Pompeii

PROCIDA
(Torre Annunziata)

SARNO RIVER

BAY OF NAPLES
Stabiae

North

CAPRI

0   5 MILES

0   10 KILOMETERS

THE VILLA DEI PAPIRI

Romans divided their busy lives into business and pleasure: *negotium* and *otium,* the former a clear negation of the latter. To remain in Rome was to face the demands of business from morning to night; pleasure was best sought elsewhere, not too far away, but not too near either. The Gulf of Naples, for many, was just right: a beautiful setting for rest and relaxation among the native Campanian population as well as in towns founded by the cultured Greeks. Naples was (and is) the largest of these towns, incorporating the early Rhodian colony of Parthenope, a name that Vergil and other poets felt free to use as a synonym for Naples, which in its original form, Nea-polis, simply and prosaically meant "new town" (like Newton and Villa Nova). There were other towns along the Bay of Naples, most notably Herculaneum (named after Herakles), Stabiae, and Pompeii, where the Romans built suburban villas overlooking the peaceful bay, and overlooked in turn by the beautiful but threatening Mt. Vesuvius (FIG. 1).

This peaceful location had long proved attractive to Greeks who here sought to re-create the famous Garden of Epikouros. The Greek philosopher Epikouros (341–270 B.C.) was the founder of a school of philosophy headquartered in the garden of his house in Athens. The followers of the school lived together in austerity, largely removed from the affairs of society. In the first century B.C., the Greek followers of Epikouros living around Naples catered to the Romans' desire for the "simple" life, especially if rich Romans were willing to act as patrons and to provide a living for their Epicurean teachers.

Thus it was that one Roman in particular, Lucius Calpurnius Piso Caesoninus, a Roman consul and senator whose daughter Calpurnia[1] married Julius Caesar, came to spend time in Herculaneum with the Epicureans Siron and, more importantly for our account, Philodemos. The latter wrote at least one poem addressed to Piso (see p. 83) and dedicated one philosophical work to him, suggesting that Piso was Philodemos's patron. Philodemos lived in a modest home (as he tells us in the poem just mentioned); Piso, most likely, lived in one of the largest villas in Herculaneum. Occasionally Piso would visit Philodemos; more often Philodemos, along with other philosophers and poets (one of them Vergil; see pp. 43f. and nn. 82, 168), would attend upon Piso in his far grander villa, all of them spending their evenings dining, drinking, and conversing.

The villa supposedly owned by Piso stood just outside the town of Herculaneum, overlooking the Mediterranean Sea. The eruption of Vesuvius in A.D. 79 buried the villa, along with the town, beneath some 20 m (65 ft.) of volcanic material. In the mid-eighteenth century the fortuitous discovery of a marble floor during well-digging led to a decade of exploration of the adjacent building. The excava-

FIGURE 1
Vesuvius seen from the ground level of modern Ercolano;
ancient Herculaneum is in the foreground. Photo: Sandra Sider.

FIGURE 2

A lifesize bronze piglet found in the Villa dei Papiri. The
Epicureans who argued for communal living were insultingly
called pigs, a term the Epicureans themselves came to find
amusing. Horace, for example, refers to himself as *Epicuri de
grege porcum,* "a pig from the Epicurean herd." Pandermalis
argued that this pig was intentionally placed near a statue of
Epikouros that dominated the entrance to the peristyle of
the Villa dei Papiri. Naples, Museo Archeologico Nazionale,
inv. 4893.

tions, carried out through underground tunnels, much as in a mining operation, were directed by a
Swiss army engineer, Karl Weber, who was employed by the king of Naples (see p. 18). In addition to
delivering written weekly reports to his superiors, Weber also drew a large plan of the structure he
encountered as the excavations progressed. From this plan we know that the Villa consisted of a very
large peristyle garden (94 x 32 m; 310 x 106 ft.) and, surrounding a smaller peristyle garden (21 x 21 m;
69 x 69 ft.), a main building that largely conformed to the plan of a classical Roman atrium house. The
driving force behind the excavation was the Villa's large collection of bronze and marble statues—at
least ninety were unearthed.[2] But it was the discovery in 1752 of a large number of charred papyrus
rolls that gave the villa its modern name: the Villa dei Papiri—the Villa of the Papyri. (When J. Paul
Getty set about building a new museum in Malibu for his collections of art, he decided that the foot-
print of his museum should be based on Karl Weber's plan of the Villa dei Papiri.)

Perhaps as many as eleven hundred papyrus rolls were excavated in the 1750s; because many were
destroyed at the time of their discovery, it is not possible to determine the original number. What is
certain is that most Greek texts were found in a single small room, the "library," but a number of rolls
were encountered scattered in various parts of the building (see FIG. 64). Most of the rolls are philosophical texts in Greek, overwhelmingly texts by the Epicurean poet and author Philodemos (ca.
110–ca. 40/35 B.C.). If, after his death, Philodemos's library became part of Piso's (as seems likely), it
remained in Herculaneum as part of Piso's estate, preserved by his heirs, who may also have been interested in Epicureanism (see pp. 7f.). And there it stayed until that August day in A.D. 79 when Vesuvius
erupted. With little warning, some people nonetheless had time to collect and escape with some of
their portable goods. In the Villa dei Papiri papyrus rolls were gathered up, although in the haste many
were left scattered on the floor. How many were removed we shall never know, but we do know that
those left behind were charred by the volcanic hot-air surges but not totally destroyed by the pyroclastic flows from the volcano.

The Villa's book rolls, like much else in Herculaneum, were preserved for far longer than would
have been the case had Vesuvius never erupted. They are, in fact, the only library from the ancient
world to survive, if not entire, then at least in large measure. The books, although not so immediately
as the art, also came to be acknowledged as a magnificent find. Opening them, however, was a problem, as was deciphering them, but soon enough they were recognized as the remains of a large

Epicurean library, as well as some works of their philosophical rivals, the Stoics. In the 1990s, fragments of the Roman Epicurean poet Lucretius were identified, along with an intriguing fragment of a Latin comedy and some truly frustrating bits of the early Roman poet Ennius.

It is this story, then, and in particular that of the library, that will be the focus of the following discussion, as we learn about the origins, contents, authors, and owners of the library.

Who Owned the Villa dei Papiri

Since the great majority of the books found in the Villa dei Papiri are Epicurean texts—and those not by Epikouros himself were mostly written by Philodemos—and since no Greek would have had the money to own such a magnificent building, it was easy if not inevitable to conclude as early as 1810 that the Villa belonged to the Roman most often associated with Philodemos as both patron and fellow Epicurean: Lucius Calpurnius Piso Caesoninus, a member of the powerful Piso family, who lived in the first century B.C. Indeed, for many years the Villa dei Papiri was called "dei Pisoni," Villa of the Piso family. Although ownership is still somewhat disputed, the links between Piso and Philodemos are secure:

(i) Philodemos addresses one of his epigrams to Piso, wittily suggesting that for his patronage Piso would in return receive from Philodemos the pleasures that only Epicureanism can bring (see pp. 81ff.).[3] The form of this epigram is that of an invitation poem; that is, Philodemos couches an invitation to a dinner in the form of a poem, a literary topos invented by Greek epigrammatists and later copied by Catullus, Horace, and other Latin poets.

(ii) In a prose treatise, *On the Good King according to Homer,* Philodemos again addresses Piso directly, an act that in a work of prose indicates that the addressee is either the author's patron or that the author wishes to receive patronage or other favor from him. Here the latter is the case, since in column 41 (two columns before Piso is named), Philodemos may be suggesting that, just as Odysseus's son Telemakhos needed guidance from Theoklymenos, so too would Piso benefit from political advice offered not only in *The Good King* but by Philodemos himself.

(iii) Cicero in his vitriolic attack against Piso—his speech *In Pisonem* of 55 B.C.—makes fun of Piso's superficial love of Epicureanism and his association with a certain Greek who is both an Epicurean philosopher and the author of erotic poetry; this can only be Philodemos. On the relation-

ship between Piso and this Greek, Cicero says: "When asked, invited, and pressed, he [the Greek] wrote reams of verse *to* Piso and *about* Piso, sketching to the life in lines of perfect finish all his lusts and immoralities, all his varied dinners and banquets, all his adulteries" (*In Pisonem* 70). In other words, there were further, no-longer-extant, poems by Philodemos on Piso. (Cicero shows a certain lack of literary finesse, however, when he reads poetry as biography.)

(iv) It has been reasonably suggested that, when Catullus attacks a member of the Piso family and two of his followers, the Piso in question is Lucius Calpurnius Piso Caesoninus and the follower given a Greek name is Philodemos, slightingly referred to here as Socration, "little Socrates" (FIG. 2).[4]

The chief evidence for locating Philodemos in Herculaneum is the library of the Villa, which, with its specialized texts and, even more, by its duplicate copies of some works by Philodemos, suggests that it was a working philosopher's library.[5] And since so many of the identified texts are by Philodemos, it is tempting to believe that this was his personal library. Furthermore, one of the texts in the collection, although lacking both title and author, contains the author's own recollections of life on the Bay of Naples: "He [unidentified in the papyrus scrap] decided to return with us to Naples and to dearest Siron [see p. 2] and his way of life there and to engage in active philosophical discourse and to live with others in Herculaneum" (*PHerc.* 312).[6] Philodemos is the most likely author of these lines.

What is altogether lacking, however, is any evidence that would connect Piso with the Villa, or even with Herculaneum. Cicero does not bother to tell his audience where Piso so closely attached himself to Philodemos, leading many to think that Rome was meant—and that, therefore, Philodemos spent much time in the capital, for which there is no explicit evidence. This absence of any evidence for Piso in Herculaneum, in particular the lack of any epigraphical evidence in the town itself, has been taken, most notably by the Roman historian Theodor Mommsen, to indicate that the Villa could *not* have belonged to Piso, since if it did, one would expect that the presence of the *gens Calpurnia* (Calpurnius family), like that of other noble Roman families in Herculaneum, would have been recorded in at least one local inscription.[7]

Thus, although most scholars agree that the evidence linking Piso with Philodemos and that linking Philodemos with Herculaneum and (through his books) the Villa does not prove Piso's ownership of the Villa, they still regard him as the most likely candidate. Only someone as rich and powerful as he could have built such a splendid dwelling. Only someone who, like Piso, had served in a position

FIGURE 3
A statue base with an inscription honoring Lucius Calpurnius
Piso, found in Samothrace. Because such honorary decrees con-
tained very formulaic language, it is easy to restore the missing
words: "The council and the People [honor] Leukios Kalpornios
Peison, the son of Leukios, the ruler and patron of the city."
Drawing: Marian Stewart.

that allowed him to amass great wealth during a stay in Greece could have furnished it on such a grand
scale (FIG. 3).[8] Indeed, Cicero makes just such a charge against Piso in two other speeches, although it
has to be said immediately that many other Romans, including Cicero himself, did all they could to
furnish their villas with art bought or seized from Greece.

Nonetheless, some other Romans have been put forward as possible owners. One scholar proposed Marcus Octavius, whose name is written toward the end of two treatises found in the Villa (one
by Philodemos, the other by Polystratos), but there is far less reason to accept ownership of the Villa
by this minor figure, a curule aedile in 50 B.C. Octavius may have been either a prior owner of the rolls
or the bookseller who placed his name in them, although parallels for this practice are lacking.

Lucius Calpurnius Piso Frugi Pontifex (FIG. 4), the son of Caesoninus, who served as consul in 15
B.C., was proposed by Dimitrios Pandermalis, who imagined a complex arrangement of the Villa's
many sculptures in bronze and marble that was in harmony with the Epicurean way of life as expound-
ed in the texts in the Villa's library.[9] The son certainly had his own literary leanings. In all likelihood
he was the Piso who, along with his two sons, was a dedicatee of Horace's famous *Art of Poetry*. One
could now close the circle by noting not only that the *Ars Poetica* draws upon literary theory found in
Philodemos's treatises on poetry but also that Horace explicitly refers to, and seems to paraphrase, an
epigram of Philodemos in one of his *Satires*.

Piso Frugi "was himself a poet and a champion of the liberal arts," as an ancient commentator on
Horace's *Ars* describes him. Like his father, he acted as patron to an epigrammatist, Antipater of
Thessalonika, who addressed several poems to him. Some of these accompanied, and described, gifts;
the most interesting is the one whose description includes the poem itself:

> Antipater gives Piso a *biblion* for his birthday, a small one, the work of but one night.
> May he though receive it graciously, with praise for the bard, just as mighty Zeus is won over
> by a small amount of incense.[10]

The complex relationship Pandermalis finds between the Villa's art and its library is not so com-
pelling as to exclude other possibilities. The date of the Villa's construction is roughly mid-first century
B.C., when Piso Caesoninus had recently returned from Greece and when Philodemos was thriving—

FIGURE 4
A bust found in Herculaneum identified as that of Lucius
Calpurnius Piso Frugi Pontifex, although it is not labeled
(see n. 11). End of first century B.C.–beginning of first century
A.D. Naples, Museo Archeologico Nazionale, inv. 5601.

FIGURE 5

Stone inscription, still in situ underground, found in the the-
ater of Herculaneum, recognizing Appius Claudius Pulcher
after his death: AP · CLAVDIO · C · F · PVLCHRO | COS · IMP |
HERCULANENSES · POST · MORT (= *Corpus Inscriptionum
Latinarum* 10.1424). Photo by and courtesy of Mario Capasso.

8

by which time, most of the Epicurean texts had already been transcribed.

Some of the papyri, however, do seem to have been produced after the death of Piso Caesoninus
(see pp. 73ff.). It thus remains possible that Piso Frugi added to his father's library because he main-
tained an interest in Epicureanism. Even if this interest extended to commissioning an interior deco-
ration scheme that was a reflection of Epicureanism, we would still be justified in thinking of Piso
Caesoninus as *the* owner; that is, the one responsible for gathering the great majority of philosophical
texts. Furthermore, what was said above, still applies: There is no actual known link between any of the
Calpurnii and Herculaneum.[11]

Another candidate for ownership is Appius Claudius Pulcher, consul in 54 B.C., whose nephew (of
the same name) was consul in 38 B.C. and who, more significantly, was the patron of the town of
Herculaneum. Claudius was, perhaps even more so than Piso, a lover of things Greek. His ties to
Herculaneum are therefore more secure than those of Piso Caesoninus, but, for all his claims to be a
man of letters and culture, he lacks Piso's ties to the Epicurean community in general and to Philodemos in particular (FIG. 5).[12]

When all is taken into account, then, Piso Caesoninus remains the most likely owner of the Villa,
and so he shall be considered here. Nonetheless, we have to keep in mind that between his death ca. 40
B.C. and the eruption of Vesuvius in A.D. 79 Philodemos's library could have been moved a number of
times. Philodemos probably never lived in the Villa (although some people believe that he did), so
there would have been no necessity for his library to have wound up there, especially when it seems
possible that he and Piso died not too far apart in time. For all of Piso's admiration for Philodemos,
therefore, he may never have taken possession of his volumes. It may even be that Philodemos had
more than one patron, any one of whom could have been the owner of the Villa.[13]

There is, after all, nothing other than the library to link Philodemos with the Villa, despite the
attempt of Marcello Gigante to interpret one of Philodemos's epigrams as referring to the belvedere
located to the west of the Villa (FIG. 6). Although the epigram does refer to the seashore, the Greek
word *apopsis,* which Gigante translates as belvedere, could just as easily be taken to refer to the
promontory on which Herculaneum was built.[14]

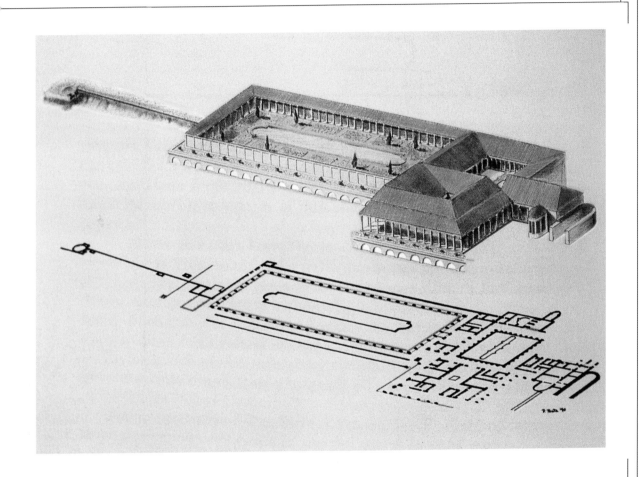

FIGURE 6
Reconstruction of the Villa dei Papiri. The papyrus rolls were
found in the far right-hand section (cf. FIG. 64). The round
structure to the far left seems to have been a belvedere, well sit-
uated for views over the Bay of Naples. Drawing: Pietro Testa.
Reproduced by courtesy of Mario Capasso.

THE ERUPTION OF
MT. VESUVIUS IN A.D. 79

Mt. Vesuvius was, and is, the only active volcano on the Italian mainland. Its last major eruption before A.D. 79 had been about 1200 B.C.;[15] the most recent series of eruptions occurred in 1944 (FIG. 7).[16] Vesuvius has sent forth noxious smoke and lava flows repeatedly without major eruption, a sight that has been captured in many paintings. In the eighteenth century, Goethe, ever the scientist, tried to get close to the crater during one such period, but was forced to retreat (FIG. 8).

Although the mountain itself was relatively calm for centuries before A.D. 79, the area west of it was known for its toxic fumes and gases. Known as the Phlegraean Fields (Gr. *phlegraios,* "flaming"), this landscape was often the death of birds owing to the ground's exhalation of carbon dioxide (see map). The Greeks called an area near Cumae *a-ornis,* "without birds," which became Avernus in Latin, another name for the underworld, as readers of Vergil's *Aeneid* will recall. The Sibyl of Cumae tells Aeneas that the "descent to the Underworld is easy" (*facilis descensus Averno; Aeneid* 6.126), but return is difficult. Undaunted, Aeneas follows her directions to "a vast chasm of jagged rocks, close by a dark lake and gloomy groves, over which opening no birds were able to fly with impunity, so great a vapor pouring forth from its black maw carried forth to the air, which is why the Greeks called the place Aornus" (*Aeneid* 6.237–42).

Between eruptions the land became fertile and welcomed in succession native Oscans, Greek colonists, and Romans who in the late fourth century B.C. appropriated these lands and towns (FIG. 9). Florus, writing his history of Rome less than a century after the eruption, had nothing but praise for Campania and its hills, calling Vesuvius the most beautiful of them all (*Epitome of Roman History* 1.11.3–6).

In the first century A.D., however, the fiery magma below Campania was stirring. In February of A.D. 62, an earthquake centered in Pompeii shook the region, causing significant damage to buildings in all the towns on the Gulf of Naples. As Seneca the Younger wrote in his *Natural Questions,* "part of Herculaneum is destroyed; even those buildings left standing are unstable" (*Quaestiones Naturales* 6.1.1–2). Since rebuilding was necessary, sculptors had the chance to portray the earthquake on the new walls (FIGS. 10, 11).[17]

Although Seneca was contemporary with the earthquake he describes, he did not see it himself; but for the eruption seventeen years later we have an eyewitness: Pliny the Younger, who described the eruption in two letters to his friend the historian Tacitus, who was gathering material to use in his his-

FIGURE 7
The last major eruption of Mt. Vesuvius, in early April 1944.
Photo: Archival Research International/Double Delta
Industries, Inc., and Pike Military Research.

tories.[18] On 24 August A.D. 79, around noon, Pliny's mother disturbed her bookish brother Pliny ("the Elder," to distinguish him from his nephew), commander of the Roman navy stationed at Cape Misenum,[19] calling him away from his studies to point out "a cloud of unusual size and appearance" coming from Vesuvius 32 km (20 miles) away across the Bay of Naples from Misenum. The cloud looked like an umbrella pine (FIG. 12), and at first its precise source was not known.[20] The Younger Pliny reports that "my uncle's scholarly acumen" was piqued; he had to see this up close. Pliny was invited to accompany his uncle but begged off: "I preferred to go on with my studies." His uncle curbed his scientific mission in order to help those stranded on the beaches below Vesuvius, ordering the warships under his command to offer passage. The nephew continues, "What he had begun in a spirit of scientific inquiry he completed as a hero. . . . He hurried to the place which everyone else was hastily leaving, steering his course straight for the danger zone. He was entirely fearless, dictating to a slave the details of each new change in the phenomena. Ashes were already falling, hotter and thicker as the ships drew near, followed by bits of pumice and blackened stones, charred and cracked by the flames." After finding a clear passage where the ship could put in, at Stabiae, it was brought quickly to shore, thanks to a wind rushing shoreward to fill the partial vacuum caused by the upward rush of air

FIGURE 8

Goethe's watercolor, made during the volcanic activity of February and March 1787. "At last I reached the old crater, now blocked, and came to the fresh lava flows. . . . I crossed it and climbed a hill of ashes which had been recently thrown up and was emitting fumes everywhere. As the smoke was drifting away from me, I decided to try and reach the crater. I had only taken fifty steps when the smoke became so dense that I could hardly see my shoes. . . . At least I now know how difficult it is to breathe in such an atmosphere" (entry of 2 March 1787, from J. W. Goethe, *Italian Journey*, trans. W. H. Auden and Elizabeth Meyer [New York, 1962]). Size: 15.8 x 19.6 cm (6¼ x 7¾ in.). Stiftung Weimarer Klassik und Kunstsammlungen, inv. KK 1292. Photo: Stefan Renno and Eberhard Renno. (Goethe's drawing, stored elsewhere, was not harmed in the unfortunate fire that destroyed much of the library in 2004.)

FIGURE 9
Vesuvius painted before the eruption of A.D. 79, which
destroyed much of the peak shown here, as well as the vegetation. Plutarch mentions that "upon the top grew a great many
wild vines" (Plutarch *Life of Crassus* 9.2, trans. John Dryden),
which were cut down to make rope ladders for Spartacus and
his fellow slaves when they were pursued by Roman forces in
73 B.C. Wall-painting from the House of the Centenary,
Pompeii. Naples, Museo Archeologico Nazionale, inv. 112286.

FIGURE 10
Marble relief from a house belonging to Lucius Caecilius
Jucundus in Pompeii depicting a detail of the earthquake
associated with the eruption of A.D. 62: One of the town
gates collapses, while a mule cart is tossed into the air.
Reproduced by kind permission of Wilhelmina Jashemski.

FIGURE 12

Postcard, ca. 1900, of a steaming Vesuvius across the Bay of Naples, viewed from a spot traditionally known as "Vergil's Tomb," near Pozzuoli and close to Cape Misenum, where the Elder Pliny was stationed. Was the photographer of this "panorama with pine tree" familiar with Pliny's description of the cloud as a pine tree? The smoke from Vesuvius has been added artifically, as was common on old postcards.

from the hot volcanic blasts. Once landed, however, the ship now faced an unfavorable wind. *Facilis descensus Averno.* The brave Pliny tried to calm his friend Pomponianus's fears by bathing and dining as if there were no threat, playing down the "broad sheets of fire and leaping flames" seen on the slopes of the mountain. He even went to bed, but his labored breathing could be heard through the door. His friends woke him when ashes and pumice stones began to fall on the open courtyards of Pomponianus's villa. The earth was shaking, so being indoors now seemed as dangerous as the hot stones falling outside. With pillows over their heads, they left as daylight, such as it was, began. Lamps were still necessary. Pliny went to the shore to find the best way to escape, but by now the sea was in turmoil, the waves too high. The air filled with smoke, ash, and sulfur proved too much for the aged Pliny's already weakened, probably asthmatic, constitution. "He stood leaning on two slaves and then suddenly collapsed." Pliny the Younger glides over some details here, but it is clear that the slaves saw no reason to carry a dead body away with them as they made their way to safety. "Two days later his body was found intact and uninjured, still fully clothed and looking more like sleep than death."[21]

Pliny's account of the eruption, much of which has been skipped here, accords with modern scientific examination, although nowadays far more can be learned than Pliny could ever have known or even thought to investigate. For our purposes, the most important thing to note is the precise nature of the fallout over Herculaneum. Because of the prevailing winds, the initial blast dropped its load of pumice southeast of Mt. Vesuvius; that is, away from Herculaneum but covering Oplontis, Boscoreale, and Pompeii (FIG. 13). This first blast, however (now called a Plinean phase, in the nephew's honor), was merely the clearing of a passage for the subsequent release of hot gases and incandescent rocks of various sizes—Pliny's "broad

NAPOLI - PANORAMA COL PINO

FIGURE 11

Another relief from Jucundus's house. As the Capitolium collapses, the statues in front, shaken out of their stone lethargy by the earthquake, throw up their arms and try to jump off their horses. Reproduced by kind permission of Wilhelmina Jashemski.

FIGURE 13

Vesuvius and nearby towns showing the areas covered with
pyroclastic material and with varying thicknesses of ash and
pumice, in cm. Drawing: Marian Stewart, based on Jashemski
and Meyer, *The Natural History of Pompeii*, fig. 33, p. 39.

14

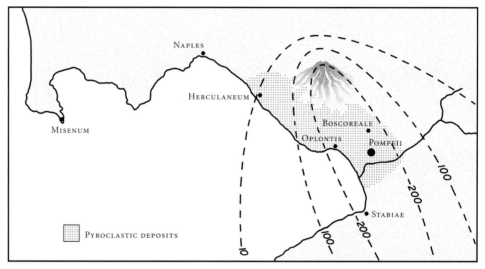

sheets of fire and leaping flames," called a *nuée ardente* (burning cloud) by vulcanologists. *Nuées
ardentes* evolve into two parts, surge and flow. The upper part of a *nuée ardente* is a low concentration
of gas and incandescent rocks called the surge. At the lower level of the *nuée ardente* is a higher concentration of the same, called the flow. Several rounds of surge and flow dropped down Vesuvius's
slopes toward Pompeii and Herculaneum with inescapable suddenness and speeds of about 100 km
(60 miles) per hour, hot enough to ignite wooden timbers, thatch, and vegetation (FIG. 14A, B). The
second pyroclastic flow deposited five feet, not only of ash, but also of whatever it had ripped off the
structures in its way, including chunks of walls, two of which weighed over a thousand pounds each.
All in all, Herculaneum was covered by six rounds of surge and flow, each one spreading farther than
the preceding. When it was over, the town lay buried under 20 m (65 ft.) of pyroclastic flow, which
became rock hard as it cooled.

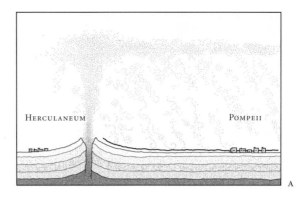

During the first stage (A) of the eruption, a column of
ash and pumice 10–15 miles high was blown away from
Herculaneum in the direction of Pompeii. When the column
partially collapsed (B), the ash and pumice began to drop
straight down, flowing along the ground and now covering
Herculaneum in alternating pyroclastic flows and surges.
Drawing: Marian Stewart, based on Jashemski and Meyer,
The Natural History of Pompeii, fig. 35, p. 42.

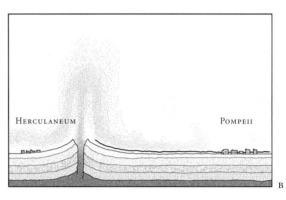

Whether surge or flow, however, pyroclastic
matter is not lava, which burns and melts.
Pyroclastic gases in either the surge or the flow
will suffocate humans and animals (one horse
was found in Herculaneum). Solid matter will
physically knock down and carry off objects
and weaker structures, and the heat will bring
things to the point of carbonization. The heat
will not, however, necessarily ignite what it covers, especially since oxygen is soon used up.
Pumice, ash, and rocks covered the Villa dei
Papiri, filling every room, but its bronze statues
were unharmed and its books were merely
charred (and dried). Whatever great trouble the book rolls have given when one tried to open them
and then to read black letters on now-dark pages (see pp. 46ff.), we must remember that the rolls
would not have survived at all if not for the eruption of Mt. Vesuvius (FIG. 15).

Vesuvius preserved what would otherwise have been destroyed. Not one medieval manuscript of
Epikouros has survived, despite the fact that he was widely read throughout the ancient Greek and
Roman world. Only because Diogenes Laertios in the third century A.D. incorporated three of
Epikouros's letters into his history of Greek philosophy are any of Epikouros's writings extant in their
entirety (see p. 96). All else are excerpts and quotations. The texts of Epikouros's writings found in
Herculaneum were not preserved in medieval manuscripts and are therefore known to us today only
because the eruption of Vesuvius preserved them.

FIGURE 15
Several charred and unopened papyrus rolls fused together
into one big lump. Photo: Sandra Sider.

Recovery of the Papyri
in the 1750s

16   A decade after the eruption, the land had not yet recovered. The Roman poet Martial wrote an eight-line epigram on the subject in A.D. 88:

> Here is Vesbius [Vesuvius], not long ago shaded by green grape vine,
>
> where the noble grape had pressed out pools of juice.
>
> Bacchus loved these acres more than his hills in Nysa.
>
> Only recently Satyrs led their dances on this mountain.
>
> 5   This was Venus' land, more pleasing to her than her temple in Sparta;
>
> this was Hercules' land, made famous by his name.
>
> All lies submerged in flames and sad ash.
>
> All the gods on high would wish such power had not been allowed them.[22]

Yet, not long after Martial wrote, the land below Vesuvius recovered its fertility and prosperity. The Neapolitan poet Statius was able to say in A.D. 95 that "Vesuvius's peak and the harsh mountain's fiery storm did not so completely extinguish the trembling cities' citizens: They stand and thrive with people."[23]

The area where Herculaneum had stood was eventually resettled, the new town taking shape on top of the old, which lay largely undisturbed for over 1600 years. Subsequent eruptions laid down even more rock and moved the coastline further out.[24] (Until recently a commercial greenhouse lay directly above the Villa dei Papiri.) Rulers came and went. As Joseph Jay Deiss nicely lists them, "with the Middle Ages came the enlightened Saracens, then the Normans, the Germans, the Angevins, the Aragonese, the Turks.... They were followed by the French, the Spaniards, the Germans, the Spaniards, the Austrians, the Bourbons, the Austrians, the Napoleonic French, the Bourbons, and the Austrians again."[25]

In 1709, when Naples was in its first Austrian phase, well-diggers in Resina found carved marble statues under the hard volcanic rock. Unwittingly they had dug into the ancient theater of Herculaneum, which became a famous tourist destination in the eighteenth and nineteenth centuries. (It is still underground today, open to visitors by appointment only.) An officer of the

FIGURE 16

Engraving by Filippo Morghen (b. 1730?), after a drawing by Camillo Paderni (ca. 1715–1781). "Charles III, King of Spain and the Indies," proclaims the circular inscription. Below, crowding the lion, are symbols of the excavations carried out while Charles was king of Naples (see FIG. 17): a portrait bust of Epikouros (cf. FIG. 65); seven papyrus rolls, some partially opened; a polyptych of five wax tablets; ceramic and metal vessels and coins; a pick and a shovel used to bring them to light; and an inscription found on a statue base in the theater of Herculaneum in which the citizens of Herculaneum honor Marcus Nonius Balbus: M · NONIO · M · F | BALBO · PR · PRO · CO[S] | HERCULANENSES (= *Corpus Inscriptionum Latinarum* 10.1426). It was inscriptions like this, with the word "Herculanenses" (citizens of Herculaneum), that enabled the first excavators to identify the town as Herculaneum (cf. FIG. 5). From *Delle Antichità di Ercolano,* vol. 1 (Naples, 1757), frontispiece. Los Angeles, Research Library, Getty Research Institute.

FIGURE 17
Detail of lower right-hand corner of figure 16. The club is an
attribute of Herakles.

Philippus Morghen Florenti. Reg. Incisor sculp.

Austrian army, Prince d'Elboeuf, took over from
the well-diggers; eager to discover more statues
with which to furnish his new villa in the nearby
town of Portici, he became the first modern
excavator of Herculaneum. Hardly a disinter-
ested archaeologist, he gave orders for lateral
tunnels to fan out underground. The illicit tunnel work continued until d'Elboeuf returned to
Austria in 1716.

In 1734 the Austrians were expelled from
Naples by the Spanish Bourbons. The new ruler
of Naples and Sicily, Charles III, soon embarked
on renewed tunnel excavations beneath Resina
(FIGS. 16, 17). In October 1738, he assigned the
task of excavating Herculaneum to the Spanish
army engineer Roque Joaquín de Alcubierre. A
century before archaeology was put on a scientific basis, Alcubierre knew only that his task was
to bring up beautiful objects. Their locations
were irrelevant, inscriptions were valueless, and
record keeping was primitive. Alcubierre essentially treated the volcanic stone of the buried city
like a rock face in a mine, something to be drilled through in one's quest for treasure. To quote Deiss
again, "The burrowing went on everywhere about the town—along streets, over roofs, through fres-
coes, mosaics, wooden doors, vaults—undermining, smashing, snatching." Or, as a contemporary
report by the famous art historian Johann Joachim Winckelmann puts it even more vividly, "This man
[Alcubierre], who, (to use the Italian proverb,) knew as much of antiquities as the moon does of lob-
sters, has been, through his want of capacity, the occasion of many antiquities being lost."[26]
Nonetheless, Alcubierre continued to oversee the excavations until 1765.

In 1750, Alcubierre was transferred to Naples, leaving the supervision of the Herculaneum excavations to another army engineer, Karl Weber of Switzerland, a hero of sorts in the history of the Villa dei Papiri. Only weeks after Weber took over, well-diggers in Resina discovered a marble floor, which Weber investigated. Following a long wall underground led him over the next years to discover the large and elegant Villa dei Papiri. Weber painstakingly took measurements throughout all of the excavation tunnels, so that he was able to draw a plan of the Villa in great detail. It is from this plan, now on display in the National Archaeological Museum in Naples, that one can easily comprehend the scale and opulence of the whole structure—even though Weber, like us today, was unable to view it with his own eyes. Even today all that is on view is one small section of the whole, exposed when in the 1990s a vast trench was dug down about 30 m (90 ft.) from the current surface (FIG. 18).

Statues of whatever size, wall-paintings, and household objects made of metal were recognized by the excavators for what they were. It took a little longer, but the papyri, too, soon became known to the world at large. Here is the first announcement in print of the discovery of books in the Villa, taken from an "extract of a letter from signor *Camillo Paderni* [director of the Museum Herculanense in the Royal Palace at Portici, where the finds from the excavations in Herculaneum were housed from the time of their discovery until they were moved to Naples between 1778 and the early 1800s] to D^r. Mead, concerning the Antiquities dug up from the antient *Herculaneum,* dated from *Naples,* Nov. 18, 1752. . . . Translated from the Italian," as printed in the (London) *Philosophical Transactions* 48.1 (1754):

> It is not a month ago [i.e., October 19, 1752], that there have been found many volumes of *papyrus,* but turn'd to a sort of charcoal, so brittle, that, being touched, it falls readily into ashes. Nevertheless, by his Majesty's orders, I have made many trials to open them, butt all to no purpose; excepting some *words,*

FIGURE 18
A view of the southern side of the Villa dei Papiri as it looks today, showing the previously unknown lower level, which remains entirely unexcavated. Photo: Sandra Sider.

which I have picked out intire, where there are divers *bits*, by which it appears in what manner the whole was written. The form of the characters, made with a very black tincture, that overcomes the darkness of the charcoal, I shall here, to oblige you, imitate two short lines; my fidelity to the king not permitting me to send you any more.

N . ALTERIUS . DVLC

DEM . CVRIS . CRVDE

This is the size and shape of the characters. In this bit there are eight lines. There are other bits with many other words; which are all preserved in order for their publication.[27]

It will be noticed that in this first announcement, Paderni chose a Latin text to excerpt, although in fact these are a small minority of the whole collection. Most of the papyri are in Greek.

In his next report to mention books (*Philosophical Transactions* 48.2 [1755]), Paderni makes an even more astonishing announcement:

> In one of these buildings there has been found an entire library, compos'd of volumes of the Egyptian Papyrus, of which there have been take out about 250; and the place is not yet clear'd or emptied, it having been deem'd necessary to erect props first, to keep the earth, which lies above it, from falling in upon it. These volumes of Papyrus consist of Latin, and Greek manuscripts; but from their brittleness, occasion'd by the fire and time, it is not possible to unrol them, they being now decay'd and rotten. His majesty however has done his part; having sent for a certain monk from Rome [Padre Antonio Piaggio; see pp. 22f.], who belong'd to the Vatican library; in hopes, by his means, to have unfolded them; but hitherto in vain.
>
> Your servant Paderni alone can shew some fragments of several lines, and more than this he is much afraid will never be seen. Of these there are many in my custody, which I suppose you will have the pleasure of observing in the intended catalogue. There have been found of those small tables, which they cover'd with wax and the *palimpseston,* and then wrote on them with the stylus: but all these are become a kind of cinder, and have likewise suffer'd by the damps; from both which circumstances they are now so tender, that they break with the touch.

Paderni's next letter cleared up what he meant by a "library." (*Philosophical Transactions* 48.2 [1755]):

> As yet we have only entered into one room, the floor of which is formed of mosaic work, not unelegant. It appears to have been a library, adorned with presses, inlaid with different sorts of wood, disposed in rows; at the top of which were cornices, as in our own times. I was buried in this spot more than twelve days, to carry off the volumes found there; many of which were so perished, that it was impossible to remove them. Those, which I took away, amounted to the number of three hundred thirthy-seven, all of them at present uncapable of being opened. These are all written in Greek characters. While I was busy in this work, I observed a large bundle, which, from the size, I imagined must contain more than a single volume. I tried with the utmost care to get it out, but could not, from the damp and weight of it. However I perceived, that it consisted, of about eighteen volumes, each of which was in length a palm and three Neapolitan inches;[28] being the longest hitherto discovered. They were wrapped about with the bark of a tree, and covered at each end with a piece of wood. All these were written in Latin, as appears by a few words, which broke off from them. I was in hopes to have got something out of them, but they are in a worse condition than the Greek. From the latter the public will see some intire columns, having myself had the good fortune to extract two, and many other fine fragments.[29] Of all these an account is drawing up, which will be published together with the other Greek characters, now engraving on copper-plates, and afterwards make a separate work by themselves [FIG. 19]. . . . At present the monk, who was sent for from Rome, to try to open the former manuscripts, has begun to give us some hopes in respect to one of them. Those which I have opened, are philosophical tracts the subjects of which are known to me; but I am not at liberty to be more explicit. When they are published, they shall be immediately conveyed to you. The first *papyri,* of which I formerly acquainted you, were in a separate room, adjoining to the beforementioned palace [i.e., the Villa dei Papiri].

Further announcements about the rolls and the attempts to unroll them were made in subsequent letters. One described that "a small bust of Epicurus with his name in Greek charactere, was found in the same room [as the papyri] . . . possibly the adornment of that part of the library, where the writings in favour of his principles were kept; and it may also be supposed, that some other heads of philosophers, found in the same room, were placed with the same taste and propriety." All these busts

FIGURE 19
Philodemos *On Rhetoric,* col. 1x. Engraving from
Herculanensium Voluminum quae supersunt (Naples, 1832) 33.
Los Angeles, Research Library, Getty Research Institute.

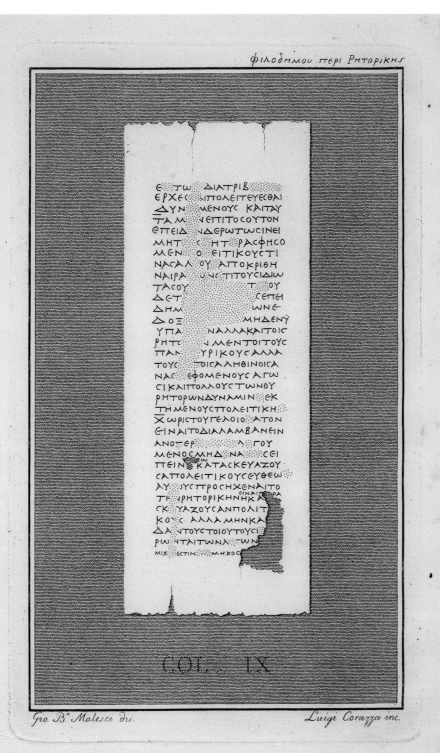

were in fact found elsewhere in the Villa (but see FIG. 65).

Paderni knew how to pique the interest of his audience. They, and soon all of erudite Europe, were intrigued as much by the new texts as by the beautiful statues, wall-paintings, and mosaics he also detailed. He glided over some mistakes on his part, however, for which he was criticized by Piaggio, as well as others. Having dropped some oblique hints in his previous letter (e.g., "I was in hopes to have got something out of [the Latin papyri], but they are in a worse condition than the Greek," which suggests that he destroyed some rolls in an attempt to open them), Paderni faced up to the criticism in a letter to Dr. Mead of 25 February 1755:

> In a chamber . . . there has been found a great quantity of rolls, about half a palm long, and round; which appeared like roots of wood, all black, and seeming to be only of one piece. One of them falling on the ground, it broke in the middle, and many letters were observed, by which it was first known, that the rolls were of papyrus. The number of these rolls, as I am told, were about 150, of different sizes. They were in wooden cases, which are so much burnt, as are all the things made of wood, that they cannot be recovered. The rolls however are hard, though each appears like one piece. Our king has caused infinite pains to be taken to unroll them, and read them; but all attempts were in vain.

It was at this point, in 1753, that Padre Antonio Piaggio (1713–1796), who had gained a reputation in the Vatican Library for his work on illuminated manuscripts, was sent for, as noted in an earlier letter. Piaggio soon learned that Paderni was not quite the heroic rescuer of the papyri he claimed to be. In Piaggio's account, which he wrote between 1769 and 1771, we read the following:[30]

> The excavators began to observe a quantity of fragments resembling carbonized wood, and when every trace of this timber was found, and these papyri resembled nothing more than wood . . . they were disregarded and left in the earth without anyone's thinking twice. Such was the lot of the first papyri, which through bad luck came to light. But when later they observed that these fragments had a consistently cylindrical form and the same dimensions, they were moved by curiosity to handle them. It was then that they considered the great delicacy of the sheets, the size and fragility of their mass, part rotted away, part carbonized. This having been established, some believed them rolls of burned cloth, others nets for fishing or

hunting, and so, breaking them with their hands or their pick-axes, they threw the fragments back into the earth, where they were mixed together and reburied without any hope of being seen again!

When Piaggio asked Paderni why this was allowed to happen, he was told:

> First: "It was not desirable to embarrass the Museum just then coming into existence and in straitened circumstances with useless things such as those which did not contain intrinsically in themselves some element of noble erudition, which were torn, or which were impossible to repair or reduce into their original form and elegance." Second: "Multiple objects are not as rare as those which are unique. . . ." The implied desecration of the papyri so lamented by me is not owed completely to the ignorance of the excavators but to their obedience and to the capriciousness of him who directs them [i.e., Paderni].

Piaggio goes on to tell how Paderni later tried to claim credit for discovering the writing: "He adds how he ran immediately to . . . Their Majesties, even though it was inconvenient, and having opened one of the rolls (that is, he cut one with a knife) in their presence, made them conceive the value of the hidden treasure he had uncovered."

At least Paderni reached a point where he saw the value in preserving these "nonunique" objects; but someone with a more genuine love of documents and with the temperament to open them, however slowly, was required before they could be read. Paderni, as we shall see, in the process of getting to a part of the rolled-up papyrus that is easier to read, simply crushed the sheets that were in his way. And then he was brash enough to criticize Piaggio for being slow: "You must intend to live too many years, if you proceed with such delicacy to discover so little."[31] Delicacy, however, is precisely what was and is required, along with many years.

THE FORM OF THE BOOK
IN GREECE AND ROME

Writing takes many forms. One can—to limit ourselves to what was available in classical Greece and Rome—scratch letters on wax, an oyster shell, or a pottery sherd (FIG. 20); or carve them in metal or stone (see FIG. 48); or one can apply a contrasting color to a suitably receptive surface, such as ink on tanned animal skin, bone (FIG. 21), wood (FIG. 22), or papyrus; or glaze on a ceramic vase (FIG. 23); or one can arrange suitably contrasting tesserae to spell out words in a mosaic, such as the famous *cave canem* found in Pompeii (FIG. 24).[32] This distinction between incising and applying contrasting coloring is not absolute, however. As the illustration of the ostrakon (see FIG. 20) shows, one can scratch through a top layer to a differently colored one below; and traces of paint within inscribed letters indicate that coloring could be added to magnify visual contrast. The boxer Diagoras of Rhodes paid for gold leaf to be laid in the letters of an inscription of the epinician (i.e., victory) ode by Pindar he had commissioned to celebrate his Olympian victory in 464 B.C. (*Olympian* 7).

Each type of lettering described above had its own range of typical uses. Wax tablets, for example, small, no more than a few inches on a side, were most appropriate for brief and temporary jottings, such as a schoolboy's assignment or an author's first draft (FIG. 25). Amazingly, many wax tablets survived the heat of Vesuvius along with some documentary papyri.[33] Curses, intended to last forever, were consigned to portable bronze or lead sheets or painted on bone. Promulgation of laws was best accomplished via stone inscriptions with letters large enough to be read by more than one person at a time. Stone inscriptions from antiquity have survived in the thousands, but we hear also of public inscriptions in media less likely to survive. Thus, Euripides tells us of the "black-lettered hides filled with the many oracles of Apollo" in Delphi.[34] Presumably, leather would stand up to constant consultation.

What was the best way of recording literary works of lasting value? For some authors, the answer lay in their memory alone. Homer and Hesiod give ample evidence of having produced poetry at the end of a long period of oral composition, when nothing was put in writing simply

FIGURE 20

Ostrakon. If enough Athenians so voted, they could send one of their fellow citizens into a ten-year exile. Even Aristeides, so upright he was nicknamed "the Just," was ostracized in 482 B.C. The ballots were oyster shells (*ostraka*) or, as shown here, broken pottery pieces, where Aristeides is identified with his father's name: ΛΥϚΙΜΑΧΟ, i.e., "(son) of Lysimakhos." Differing from the letter forms adopted later in the century are the "three-bar sigma" (which later became the four-bar variety: Σ), lambda, and upsilon. Note, too, the misspelling of Aristeides' name with two sigmas. Sixty-eight ostraka bearing Aristeides' name have been found in the Athenian Agora alone (see Mabel L. Lang, *The Athenian Agora*, vol. 25, *Ostraka* [Princeton, 1990]). Max. dim. 11.5 cm (4½ in.). American School of Classical Studies at Athens, inv. P 20399. Photo © Agora Excavations.

FIGURE 21

Polished bone on which a curse in the Coptic language
has been painted, ninth–tenth century A.D. Detail. Milan,
P.Mil.Vogl. collection. Photo courtesy of Claudio Galazzi.

FIGURE 22

Detail of a wooden board from Egypt on which were written,
in the sixth or seventh century A.D., a number of lines of
Homer's *Iliad*. The wood was covered with ochre paint
before the letters were applied. On this side the same line
was written nineteen times; on the other, with many errors,
Book 7, lines 21–28. (See Ann E. Hanson, "Iliad VII.21–28
and II.244 on a Wooden Board at Fordham University, New
York," *Papyrologica Florentina* 18 [1989] 169–73.) New York,
Fordham University, University Libraries, Special Collections
inv. T 1/82. Photo: Sandra Sider.

because there *was* no way to record words other than in living memory, in that of the composer and of his audiences. Even after writing had come to Greece from the Semitic East, a poet might write verses on papyrus (whether or not composing with pen and ink in hand), but "publication" was in the future—however that term is to be understood in the ancient world. Nor would the poet ever consider reciting while holding a text (although centuries later precisely this pose became the standard way to identify the subject of a statue as a poet or orator).[35] Still, even if Sappho wrote only one copy of each of her poems, we know what form this took: the papyrus roll, the same form books would have for centuries to come.

We should begin, therefore, by describing the form of the ancient book and distinguishing this from the image that the word *book* brings to mind nowadays. The modern book has pages bound, whether by sewn stitches, glue, or staples, along one vertical side—pages which are made by felting relatively short fibers of vegetable matter, typically wood fibers, although cotton, linen, and mulberry paper may still be found. The ancient book, in contrast, was a roll of papyrus, so that in both form (roll, not codex) and substance (papyrus, not paper) the ancient book was markedly different from what we now think of when we hear this word. The Greek *biblos* or *khartes* (Latin *charta*)[36] was a scroll (or roll) typically 13–30 cm high (5–12 in.) and as long as was necessary to contain its text, like a Torah, microfilm, or videotape.[37]

The papyrus plant (*Cyperus papyrus*) is a reed that, especially in its native environment in the water along the banks of the Nile, can easily grow 4.5 m (15 ft.) tall and 7.5 cm (3 in.) in diameter (see frontispiece). Theophrastos, Aristotle's most famous student, describes it as follows in his *History of Plants* 4.8.3:

FIGURE 23

Part of a schoolroom scene. An older student is writing with a stylus onto a waxed tablet, here seen edgewise. The stylus is sharp at one end for incising in the wax and flat at the other to smooth away words no longer needed. The inscription partially visible above the figures says "Hippodamas is beautiful." For another scene from this cup, see FIG. 45. The scene is interpreted in Barry B. Powell, *Writing and the Origins of Greek Literature* (Cambridge, 2002) 138–40. Detail of an Attic drinking cup from around 480 B.C. Berlin, Antikensammlung, inv. F 2285. Photo: Bildarchiv Preussischer Kulturbesitz/Art Resource, NY.

FIGURE 24
Cave Canem (Beware of the dog) mosaic still in its original
place in the floor of the entrance to the House of the Tragic
Poet in Pompeii. Photo: Scala/Art Resources, NY.

> The papyrus does not grow in deep water, but only in a depth of about two cubits [90 cm; 3 ft.] and
> sometimes shallower. The thickness of the root is that of the wrist of a stalwart man, and the length
> above four cubits; it grows above the ground itself, throwing down slender matted roots into the mud,
> and producing above the stalks which give it its name "papyros"; these are three-cornered and about ten
> cubits long, having a plume which is useless and weak, and no fruit whatsoever; and these stalks the
> plant sends up at many points.[38]

Thanks to Pliny the Elder's detailed account in his *Natural History* 13.74–82, as well as from modern papyrus manufacturers, we know how papyrus was prepared. Papermakers peeled away the tough
outer rind, cut the stalks to size, and peeled or sliced the underlying pith, in order to produce the
widest possible strips (FIG. 26). Next they set out a layer of fibers parallel to each other with minimal
overlap; on top of this layer, at ninety degrees, they set out a cross-layer of parallel strips (FIG. 27).
These two layers, still moist and somewhat sticky, were put in a press until
they formed one unit as the vascular fibers on the two surfaces were
crushed against each other to form a velcrolike join. Next they were left out
to dry in the sun, where they could make a sound like thunder when they
were rattled by the winds.[39] The dried sheet, trimmed to an appropriate
size, was called a *kollema,* which translates loosely as "glued unit," although
no extra adhesive is necessary. When the *kollemata* were fully dried, the pale
cucumber green of the pith had faded to a very light brown, although some
fibers remained darker than others, a fact that today proves useful to papyrologists, who are sometimes able to use the variously colored fibers like a
bar code that offers clues as to which scraps align with which.

On the side with horizontal fibers, those sheets designed for writing[40]
were rubbed smooth with a straightedge made of ivory or seashell.[41] Pliny
and Isidore of Seville give us a seven-step grading scheme for papyri, rang-
ing from *augusta* (the best) to *emporitica* (the cheapest). *Kollemata* of the
same height and somewhat the same width, laid so that the horizontal
fibers were all facing the same way, were joined by overlapping one *kollema*
slightly with another along their vertical edges. This overlap (the *kollesis*) is

FIGURE 25
Double portrait of Terentius Neo and his wife. He holds an
official documentary papyrus roll with a wax seal. She, in a
pose that is typical of wall-paintings of women in this period,
thoughtfully holds the end of a stylus to her mouth while
holding a waxed tablet (here a triptych—three tablets bound
together). See Felice Costabile, "Il ritratto di Terentius Neo
con gli instrumenta scriptoria," *Minima Epigraphica et
Papyrologica* 3 (2000) 8–17. Wall-painting, from Pompeii.
Naples, Museo Archeologico Nazionale, inv. 9058.

about 1 cm (3/8 in.) wide.[42] Since by now the natural stickiness of the pith was lost, adhesion at the *kollesis* was attained by means of paste. As Pliny tells us, this was made of flour and water, which was allowed to set for a day. A little vinegar was added to impede the growth of mold in the warm Egyptian climate.[43] The four layers of the *kollesis* were hammered so smooth that it is often difficult to see where one *kollema* ends and the next one begins. Scribes regularly wrote across the *kolleseis* (FIGS. 28, 29).

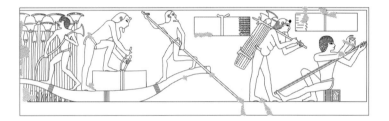

Since a book could readily comprise more than the twenty *kollemata* that were considered standard, and could thus easily attain lengths of 9 m (10 yds.) and often more, the only practical way to hold and store one was to roll it up.[44] The writing always faced inward so that it would not be subjected to rubbing or other sources of damage if put down without being rewound to the beginning.[45]

The side of the scroll that faced outward was usually left blank, especially when the roll contained literary or otherwise important texts. To provide further protection when the text was wound back to its opening lines, the first sheet (or so) was kept blank, although this *protokollon* could also be used to authenticate an official document or otherwise describe its contents; hence, at some remove of meaning, English "protocol."

It helped to attach one or both vertical edges to a wooden stick a little longer on top and bottom than the height of the roll. The projecting knobs, and then the entire wooden stick, was called the *umbilicus* (navel) in Latin. Several *umbilici* have survived in Herculaneum and elsewhere (FIG. 30).[46] "To unwind" a book in Greek and Latin meant "to read" it. "To unroll to the *umbilicus*" meant "to read a book all the way through to the end."

Romans stored rolls either vertically in containers like umbrella stands (FIG. 31) or horizontally on shelves (see FIG. 63). The identification of the contents of the rolls was made easier by attaching a protruding tag (*sillybos*) to the outside top edge of the papyrus to identify the contents, just like the spine of a modern book. Many such tags are extant, often detached from scrolls now lost; perhaps the

FIGURE 26

A continuous narrative from a fourteenth-century-B.C. wall-painting in an Egyptian tomb showing, from left to right, various stages in the preparation of objects (not all of them writing surfaces; see n. 40) made from papyrus: picking the stalks along the Nile from a boat, transporting the cut stalks by boat and then on land, and peeling the stalks to the correct thickness. Drawing: Marian Stewart.

FIGURE 27
Vertical and horizontal strips of modern papyri separated
in order to demonstrate the structure of a papyrus sheet.

most heartbreaking for a lover of Greek poetry is the *sillybos* that reads *Pindaros holos*, "The Complete
Works of Pindar" (FIG. 32).[47]

So far we have described what could be a blank roll. It is time to write on it. For a literary text you
would want to obtain the services of an accomplished scribe. If you were in the publishing business,
you would want several scribes, so that from one dictation of a text, more than one copy could be made
simultaneously. The scribe would come prepared with his ink pot and pen (FIGS. 33, 34). The ink was
a simple mixture of carbon black (soot), derived from burnt lamp wicks; gum arabic, a sticky substance derived from acacias and other trees; and enough water to attain the proper consistency. Carbon
ink is unaffected by light and is so stable that it remains legible even after two millennia, although, as
we shall see, problems arise when the papyrus is blackened by heat, as happened in Herculaneum.
Carbon ink, however, is also, as its recipe indicates, soluble in water. Some of the Herculaneum papyri
lost letters even before charring because of the steam produced during the eruption or from the mud
that later covered the area.[48]

The scribe would now take his pen (*calamus*, see FIG. 34), which was cut from a hard reed, and
write while sitting cross-legged on the ground and holding the papyrus steady on a flat surface

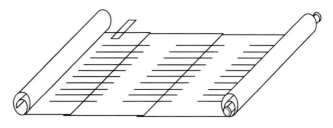

stretched across his knees, or more simply across
his skirt stretched tight between his legs (FIG. 35),
although stools and writing tables are not
unknown later in the ancient world. The scribe
would also have sponge and water handy to erase
errors. The Latin poet Martial once wrote to a
friend that he was sending a sponge along with
his latest book so that any offending poems
could be erased (Martial 4.10); in another poem
he apologizes for having sent out his servant
with a book that got drenched in a rain shower,
but then says that that is the way his book *ought*
to be sent (3.100).

The last sheet of the roll sometimes con-

FIGURE 28
Schematic drawing of a partially opened papyrus scroll,
showing the joins (*kolleseis*) between sheets (*kollemata*,
khartai). Note that the joins are so smooth that the writing
(represented here by horizontal lines) can easily pass over
them. Note, too, the *sillybos* pasted on so that the title can
be written on the part that extends beyond the roll. Cf.
FIGS. 29, 32. Drawing: Marian Stewart.

FIGURE 29
Papyrus whose *kollemata* are no longer the same color, which
clearly demonstrates how scribes often wrote across joins.
Oxford, Sackler Library, *P.Oxy.* LXIII 4358. Photo: Author.

FIGURE 31
Engraving of a wall-painting from Pompeii. In the center is
a *capsa*, a kind of bucket designed for holding papyrus rolls
(note the *sillyboi*), with a lid and straps for easy carrying.
Leaning against it is a whitened tablet with indecipherable
Latin letters, half written in one direction, half at right
angles. At left is a diptych—two (closed) wax tablets. From
Delle antichità di Ercolano, vol. 2 (Naples, 1759), pl. ii, p. 7.
Los Angeles, Research Library, Getty Research Institute.

tained an end-title (L. *subscriptio*), so that, if some lazy reader neglected to rewind the book, both beginning and end of a roll could identify title and author.[49] Few initial titles have been preserved on the Herculaneum papyri, for they suffered the greatest damage on their outer surfaces, where the text begins. Indeed, for a long time it was thought that there were no initial titles.[50] Before the practices described here became common, the author himself would begin with a first sentence that essentially served as title page. Thus Herodotos begins his *Histories* as follows: "This is the publication of the *Investigations* of *Herodotos* of *Halikarnassos* . . . ," where the underlined words would now be found on the spine and title page—and the rest of this long first sentence describes the contents in a way that would go nicely on the dust jacket: " . . . in order that the great and remarkable deeds of both Greeks and foreigners not be lost in time and go unreported, in particular the causes of the war they waged against each other."

Since a roll has no pages, it was necessary to write in columns. (In Greek a column is a *selis*, pl. *selides;* in Latin a *pagina*.) In writing down Homer or another poet, the scribe would let the metrical line length determine the column's width. Line lengths for prose were up to the individual scribe, but an average length is about three inches. An experienced papyrologist has noted that "oratory is often written in narrower columns than history or philosophy,"[51] although it is difficult to guess why this should be so. Both papyrus columns and lines were often numbered, and sometimes *kollemata* were as well. Among the Herculaneum papyri, for example, Philodemos's *On Gratitude* ends with a line count of XXXHHHHⲄΔ = 3460, a *kollema* count of ϘE = 95, and a column count of PΛZ = 137.[52] A papyrus of a lyric poem of Stesikhoros published in 1967 surprised scholars with the line number N = 1300; they had had no idea that fifth-century lyric poems were so long. In another newly discovered papyrus, a third-century-B.C. epigram book by Poseidippos, each topical section ("shipwrecks," "gemstones," etc.) comes with its own line count; in addition, every tenth line is marked off by a marginal dot and the end of each epigram by a *paragraphos,* a simple horizontal line beginning in the margin and extending a short distance into the block of text. With these visual markers the reader can easily spot a text with missing lines (FIG. 36).

The *paragraphos* was also used to mark off sections of poems, the beginning of a quotation, or, in drama, the change from one speaker to another. Some scribes preferred a more elaborate marker called a coronis. As the Greek name (*koronis,* "crow's beak") shows, these markers began as distinctly

FIGURE 30
Broken wooden *umbilicus* from a Herculaneum papyrus
roll. Photo courtesy of Mario Capasso.

curved lines, but in time took on a life of their own as scribes let their hands run free. An especially attractive coronis marks the end of a lyric strophe in one of the earliest Greek papyri known, that of Timotheus's late fifth-century poem on the Persian Wars earlier that century (FIGS. 37, 38).[53]

When the scribe had finished his task, the book was ready to be sold or presented as a gift. All that remained was to scrape smooth the upper and lower edges with pumice and, for a deluxe edition, to dust the edges with colored powder (FIG. 39).

HOW TO READ A BOOK ROLL (AND HOW NOT TO)

Reading a book roll required two hands. They need not be your own, though. Pliny the Elder, for example, was so thirsty for knowledge that he had slaves read to him morning, noon, and night, during all of his daily activities, including his bath.[54] Similarly, an Attic vase of the mid-fifth-century B.C. shows one woman reading aloud to another (FIG. 40). But whoever reads the text must simultaneously unroll the book with the right hand while the left hand rolls up the part of the scroll already read (FIG. 41). All that strictly needs to be visible at one time is one column, although in practice two or three were probably on view. A wall-painting from Pompeii shows a woman so obviously caught up in her reading that she cannot be bothered to coordinate rolling and unrolling (FIG. 42). Or is it rather that the artist exaggerated because he liked the languid swoop of the roll as it crossed the similar drape of her garment? Note too the unrealistic ∫-curve of the roll, which means that, although she is rolling the writing side so that it will be protected, the papyrus to begin with had been rolled so that the writing was on the outside. Nor is this the only artist to depict an ∫-curve rather than the correct form that

FIGURE 32

Sillybos, first century A.D.: CωΦPONOC MIMOI ΓYNAIKEIOI, "Sophron's mimes with women (characters)." Note the empty space to the right, where the tag would have been pasted to the text. In the fifth century B.C., Sophron wrote dramatic dialogues called mimes, which some, but not Philodemos, considered poetry. Papyrus, 2.8 x 12.5 cm (1⅛ x 4⅞ in.). London, The British Library, *P.Oxy.* 301.

FIGURE 33
Octagonal bronze inkpot from the House of Oppius Gratus
in Pompeii. First century A.D. Naples, Museo Archeologico
Nazionale, inv. 115614. Photographer: Catapano.

a partially unrolled book takes. A wall-painting from Herculaneum shows the reverse error: a young man rewinding the scroll so that the writing will be exposed (FIG. 43).

A well-known Greek vase shows the poet Sappho winding and unwinding a scroll correctly; it also has her sensibly resting her arms and the scroll on her legs, which must have been common (FIG. 44). The painter has taken the trouble to write some (but not all) intelligible words: "Gods! Of high-flying verses I begin [some nonsense letters follow]."[55] The painter has also repeated two of these words on the outer side of the papyrus, reading vertically down on the rolls: ΗΕΡΙΩΝ on the left and ΕΠΕΩΝ, on the right. Perhaps this otherwise careful artist intends "high-flying verses" to serve as a label for Sappho's verses in general. It is worth pointing out, with Immerwahr, how often fifth-century vase-painters show women reading. They may not have attended schools, but there can be no doubt about the literacy of at least upper-class women.[56]

Another unrealistic depiction has the text on the books running parallel to the roll, as on a vase painted by Douris (FIG. 45). In one part of a classroom scene that goes all around the vase, a seated teacher holds up a roll before a standing student, on which we can read the beginning of an otherwise unknown poem in the same hexameter meter as that used by Homer: "Muse, to me—I begin to sing about the swiftly flowing [Trojan river] Scamander." We can pardon the artist his somewhat shaky syntax. We can also understand why he has written the lines of Greek parallel to the rolls of the book. Wanting the text to be as legible as possible to the viewer of the vase, and probably not having mastered

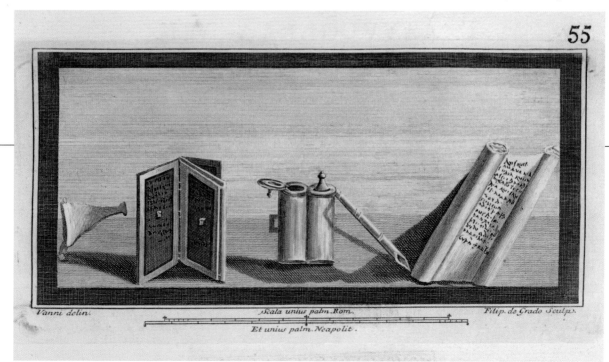

55

Vanni delin.   Scala unius palm. Rom.   Filip. de Grado Sculps.

Et unius palm. Neapolit.

FIGURE 35

Egyptian scribe seated in the usual pose with a papyrus roll
held across his lap, from Saqqara. Fifth Dynasty, 2465–2323
B.C. Painted limestone. Paris, Musée du Louvre, inv. AE/N 2290.
Photo: © Réunion des Musées Nationaux/Art Resource, NY.
Photographer: Hervé Lewandowski.

the skill of showing letters in perspective (a problem ignored by the painter of Sappho), Douris
simply presents the opened book flat in the vertical plane. Turning the letters sideways allows for a
more realistic way for the teacher to hold the
book, although it also blurs the point of the lesson. Probably we should understand him to be holding
the book so that only he can see the text while the student recites its text from memory. Another example of a depiction of sideways writing is on a fragmentary cup of the early fifth century (FIG. 46), where
again we can read a mildly imperfect poetic tag: "Leading the song set for the chorus," where the par-
ticiple *leading* has as its unexpressed grammatical subject a female chorus.[57] That the artist has the viewer of the vase in mind is even clearer from a fragment in the Getty Museum, where the boy holds the
roll correctly but the words are set at 90 degrees (FIG. 47).

ANCIENT BOOKS AND LIBRARIES

Although the form taken by the book changed over the course of time, it is important to realize that
books, indeed writing, did not always exist. In the Mycenaean age (about 1200 B.C.), a crude form of
writing was adapted from another (as yet unidentified) language in order to write Greek. This writing
was used mostly to record property, and not for continuous narratives of any sort.

Culture does not require writing; it does, though, benefit from the continuity provided by the
transmission from one generation to the next all that this particular society finds useful—everything
from the techniques of farming, building, and sailing, to the ethical practices that keep people from
harming each other and the penalties to inflict when they do. In general, then, the more successful and
traditional an oral culture is, the greater its reliance on memory. In Greece, this memory was often
stored in the form of hexameter verses, which could be recalled if not all of it by everybody, then by
those entrusted by the community: clan leaders in positions of power, who would be called upon to
recall similar situations that could help decide a matter. Jeremiah 26 provides a biblical example:
Jeremiah, having delivered yet another jeremiad, is brought under threat of death before the "elders of
the land," who cite precedents on both sides—Micah, who was not punished for prophecies similar to

FIGURE 34

Engraving of a wall-painting showing, at left, a detailed *sillybos*
(cf. FIG. 63) and a wax tablet with the wooden bosses that kept
the facing wax surfaces from touching each other when the
triptych was closed. In the center is a double inkpot, on which
leans a reed pen (Gr. *kalamos*, taken into L. as *calamus*), with
(although it is hard to discern) a split end to hold the ink.
At right, an opened papyrus roll with nonsense letters. From
Delle antichità di Ercolano, vol. 2 (Naples, 1759), pl. IX, p. 55.
Los Angeles, Research Library, Getty Research Institute.

ΕΞΙΕΓΓΥΑΝΙΚΑΙ... ΕΤΟΥΤΟΜΕΤΑ

ΝΑΥΑΤΙΚΑ

ΑΠΙΕΙΚΑΤΤΕΦΑΛΑΙΝΟΞΕΝΟΣΤΑΦΟΣΩΤΟΣΚΛΟΝΤΕΙ
ΛΛΚΡΕΧΕΙΡΚΑΙΘΕΟΙCΙΕΜΠΕΡΑΔΙΟΙΕΤCΛΘΕ
ΤΟCΕΛΑCΑΛΜΕC... ΕΤΡΕ... ΛΠΟΝΟΕCΤΟΡΙCΑC
ΑΕΤΑΙΚΑΙΤΕΑΙΟΝΙΚΥΑΛ
ΩΛΕCΕΝΑΡΧΕΔΝΑΚΟΡΗ
ΕΡΥΓΟΝΕΝΑΙΓΔΡΩΙΝΙΠCΟΜΕΝΟΙ
ΗΝΕΝΕΕΛΠCΕΙCΔΕΚΕCΕΝΛΡΩC... ΕΝΟΝΑΛΛΩC... ΕCΤΕ
ΛΙCΤΑCΛΛΗCΕΩΔΕCΥΦΑΛΛΣΡΟΡΚΕΟΝΤΕCΑΛΙΩΝ
ΟΕΤΟCΚΙΔ... ΑΤΕΓΕΛΤΟΚΑΙΕΝΤΟΤΕCΗΓΛΥΤΟΛΟΙCΙΥ
ΜΕΤΑΥΓΕCΤΕΤΕΛΕΝΑΥΤΙΝΕCΤΩΝΤΟΤΟΡΟC
ΤΟΥΤΟΝΙΛΟΥΚΕΝΕΟΝΛΕΡΟΥΤΑΓΗΝΟΝΤΡΑΦΑΝΕΩΝ
ΓΗΔΕΜΕΝΕCΙΚΑΙΛΟΙΝΕCΕΧΟΥCΙΝΑΛΟC
ΝΗΟCΑΤΟΛΑΥΜΕΝΛΤΕCΓΡΑΤΕΩΛΕΤΟΤΕCΑCΩΕΡΟC
ΝΑΥΟΤΕCΝΗ...
ΓΙΤΤΛΡΤΕΛΑ... ... ΛΛΙΜΕΝΩΝ
ΜΡΟΜΕΝΟΡ...
ΤΟΤΕΧΡΙCLΤΟΝ... ΓΕΕΡΑΛΝΟΥΤΟΥΤΟΓΕΤΕΡΟΛΛCΕΛΛΛΝΑ
ΙΕΙΕΡΕΝ... ΕΤΟΤΑΡΤΥΧΙΟΝΕΤΕΚΗ...ΟΚΕΡΩ
ΒΩΝCΛΙΤΟΥΤΙCΕΤΕΛΛΟΝΤΟΤΤΟΥΤΑΤΕΡΕΙΔΕΙΓΚΕΥΓΕΤΕ
ΛΡΠΛ... ΚΤΟΝΗΗΑΜΝΕΧΘΕCΕΤΕΡΓΙΟΝΑ
ΕΝΤΕΤΕΡΙΒΛΙΝΟΜΕΝΩΙΓΕΓΜΙΤΕCΚΑΙΤΟΤΟΝCΕΡΝΩCΧΡΗ
ΤΟΤΤΡΗ... ΗΤΙCΟΝΤΟΥΑCΤΡΟΤΛΡΤΙΑΤΕΩ
ΗΛΥΙCΤΟΝΜΕΘΑΝΟΝΤΑΚΑΙΕCΛΛΥCΕΝΛΙCΥ
ΧΕΙΡΛΡΑΝΤΟCCΤΟΥ... ΙΝΚΛΥΤΟCCΕΡ... ΕΠCΑΛΕCΘΕ
ΕΩCΑΝΕCΤΙΞΕΝΤΕΚΛΙΟΔΟΤΤΟΡΟCΑΛΛΛΜΕΔΟΥΓΕΛΛ
ΛΕCΩΛΑC... ... ΜΕΓΛΛΛΤΩΝΜΙΚΛCΕΙ...Ι... ΡΙΤΑ

ΙΑΜΑΤΙΚΑ

ΟΙΟCΟΛΛΗΞΕΝΟCΕΗΤΑCΕΤΟCCΕΛΛΕΙΤΤΗΛΛΠCΑΙΩΝ
ΤΗΕCΗCΙΛΗ... ... ΝΛΡ... ΝΟΜΜΑΤΙCΓΡΑΕΙ... ΘΙ
ΕΤΗΟΥΓΕΥΠΕCΑCΕΙ... ΤΟΥΕΝΤΑΞΕΙΝΑΛΙΕΩCΕΕ
ΔΙΤΕΛΙΔΩ... ΙΛΝ... ΡΕΕΙΝΑCΤΓΙΟΟCΕΥΓΛΙΕΝΛ...
ΝΗCΔΕΡΙCΛΛΛΙΤΕΩΝΟCΑΛΝΟΙΟCΩΤΕΝΙΝΙΚΗ
ΤΗΝΙΛΚΑΗΓΡΛΔΩΝΡΕΔCΛΝΕΩ... ΡΕΛΤΗC
CΟCΕΩΤΕΓΕΛΤΕΑΛΛΟΝΕΙCΙΝΥΡΙCΗΝΤΗΡΕΛΝΤΕ
ΛΕΙΓΛΝΟΙΛΝΕΡΟΥΤΕΓΥΤΟΝΛ... ΕΘΕΤCΕΙCΕΑC... ΛΝ
ΤΕΡΟCΕCΕΛΛΕΝΛΛΛΤΥΧΙΔΟΤΕCΔΕΚΛΛΤΙCΕΓΥΝΛΥCΙΒΙΕ
ΙΛΕΞΕΛΛΤΥΡΟΤCΓΥΤΥΤΝΕΝΟCΕ... ΓΕΛΚΟΛΕΜΟC

FIGURE 36
Column of a papyrus containing epigrams of Poseidippos, which have been arranged by subject. The first line in the column is the last line of the section on horses (*hippika*) and is numbered 98 (ἰη´). The next section, on shipwrecks (*nauagika*), contains six poems, each (except the last one) marked off at the end by a *paragraphos*, a horizontal line in the left margin extending somewhat into the text. Every tenth line is marked by a small bullet (·), and at the end there is a total line count for the section, 26 (κϛ´). The following section is dedicated to poems on illness (*iamatika*). Milan, *P.Mil.Vogl.* VIII 309, col. XIV. Photo courtesy of Claudio Galazzi.

Jeremiah's, and Urijah, who was killed. Fortunately for Jeremiah, the precedent of Micah carried the day. In Greece, rulers or elders with judicial powers were sometimes called *mnemones* or *hieromnemones,* that is, "memorizers" or "sacred memorizers." Hesiod, Homer's younger contemporary, shows that these magistrates originally memorized precedents in hexameter form.

What happens to the old-fashioned way of doing business when new technology—in this case writing—comes along? The second time the Greeks adapted writing, in the eighth century B.C., it was from Phoenican traders with whom they now had frequent contact. The Phoenician script (similar to that of its fellow-Semitic language Hebrew) has symbols for consonants only. It was the brilliant innovation of the Greeks to modify some of these to represent pure vowel sounds.

It may not be an accident that the one episode in all of Homer that refers to writing is hardly favorable.[58] Bellerophon is sent to Lycia (now in Turkey) by King Proitos, who "handed him murderous symbols, which he inscribed in a folding table, enough to destroy life, and told him to show it to his wife's father, that he might perish" (*Iliad* 6.168–70, trans. Richmond Lattimore). These "baleful signs" (*semata lugra*) may be a hazy memory of Greece's earlier alphabet in the Mycenean age; they may also reflect Homer's own feelings about the nature of these signs, which can destroy not only men but also the need for professional *mnemones,* as indeed turned out to be the case. From this time on (which may have been the early eighth century B.C.), poets wrote down their texts, which were then, as before, to be memorized for performance. A "poetry reading" would have been unthinkable. Bards who composed extemporaneously on the scale of Homer, however, were no more. Memory, hitherto solely a mental function, had now been externalized and made more permanent in the form of writing. As Prometheus says in *Prometheus Bound* when listing all that mankind owes to him: "I gave them the putting-together of letters [= writing] as memory of all things."[59] Similarly, the supposed human inventor of writing, the mythical Palamedes, says that he "invented vowels, consonants, and syllables as a drug against forgetfulness. . . . Thus, the sailor away at sea can get news from home and fathers can specify precisely in a will what his sons are to inherit. The written word will do away with all the evils that come to men when they disagree; it will not allow lies." This last sentence, as Euripides who wrote it knew all too well, is a little optimistic.[60]

Moreover, if writing could preserve what had earlier had to be stored in living memory in poetic form, poetry itself lost its status as the preserver of the group's history and mores. Prose could serve

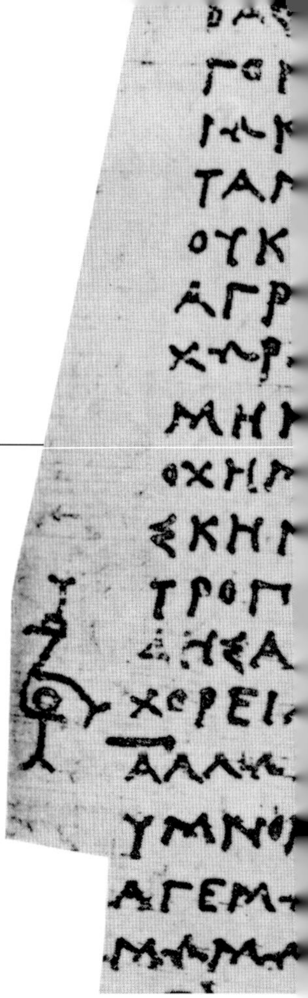

FIGURE 37
The left-hand side of a fourth-century-B.C. papyrus containing *The Persians*, a lyric poem by Timotheus (fifth century), showing two stanzas separated by a *paragraphos*, which is all that is needed, and an elaborate colophon in the shape of an ibis about to bring forth an egg. Note the use of inscription-like (lapidary) letters in this, one of the earliest Greek papyri extant. Berlin, *P.Berol.* 9875, col. v. From B. A. van Groningen, *Short Manual of Greek Palaeography* (Leiden, 1955), pl. 1.

just as well. Pherekydes of Syros, for example, credited by the Greeks with having been the first to write in prose (when they weren't crediting Anaximander of Miletos), wrote an elaborate prose cosmogony with obviously allegorical gods to explain the origin of seasons and human practices.[61] Earlier, any such composition, whether by Hesiod (a historical figure) or Orpheus (who was not), would have been in hexameters.

Perhaps more indicative of prose's new status is the story about the pre-Socratic philosopher Herakleitos's having deposited his prose text in a temple for safekeeping (see n. 53). He clearly thought that his words had to be seen exactly as he had written them in order for the full force of their ambiguity to be felt. Here we have a real-life parallel to what we read in the introduction to the Gilgamesh epic, which says that Gilgamesh wrote down "all his labours on a tablet of stone" and placed it in a "tablet-box of cedar," which he seems to have deposited in or on the wall of Uruk, the city he had built.[62]

In Greece the book never held the same sacred status it had among Jews and later among Christians and Muslims, but its power to influence human behavior was never underestimated. For the most part, the written text coexisted comfortably with the still pervasively oral culture. People spoke of "hearing" a text that had clearly been read. Perhaps this was a term that remained frozen, just as we may refer to steel knives, forks, and spoons as silverware, and we still speak of dialing a phone number; or perhaps it was because it was a long-standing Greek habit to read a text aloud even when alone.

It is an indication of the growing significance of books that they entered the realm of metaphor. From the fifth century B.C. onward, one finds the notion of the "mind's tablets" for memory. Plato used this most effectively in his *Theaitetos,* where Sokrates tested and found wanting the idea that knowledge was simply recalling what had been impressed in the mind's wax tablet. First, just like real wax tablets, memory can get dirty and no longer hold a clean image, and is thus imperfect; second, in line with Herakleitos, knowledge calls for more than mere recollection.

As we approach the Hellenistic age (which officially begins with the death of Alexander the Great

FIGURE 38
Coronis marking the end of Philodemos *Rhetoric, PHerc.* 1426, col. 16a. Drawing: Marian Stewart.

in 323 B.C.), it is hard to find anybody not enamoured of books. Public libraries are established in Athens, Alexandria, and Pergamon, to name only the more famous ones, and there is evidence for libraries throughout the Greek world.

Although still in roll form in the Hellenistic age, books were now very much the kind of object we are familiar with: things to collect, read, annotate, edit, make fun of, take seriously, and list among one's property in a will. The most famous case of a library passing from one person to another is the collection amassed by Aristotle, who willed it, not to his school (which may not have been possible legally), but to his ablest student, Theophrastos, who in turn willed it to Neleus, who took the books, surely against Theophrastos's original intentions, back to his home in Skepsis in the Troad in 285 B.C. There they remained in his family's possession (buried for a time, it is said, so as not to have them seized by King Attalos for his library in Pergamon), until they were sold to Apellikon ("a booklover rather than philosopher," says Strabo), who returned them to Athens ca. 100 B.C. and had them copied and published. Then they were seized by the rapacious Sulla, who took them, along with many works of statuary, to Rome, where they were edited and studied. A fine story, even if not true in all its details.[63]

If someone wished to buy a book, he would simply go to a nearby bookseller. In Athens, for example, the booksellers' tables could be found in the Agora, the ancient town square that served as the center of both civil and mercantile activities. When Sokrates wished to learn what Anaxagoras had written, he bought a copy for two drachmas. Were booksellers so well stocked that they would keep all the pre-Socratics on their tables? Perhaps in response to Sokrates' request the bookseller had a copy made from a master copy: a form of publication on demand.

There are ancient testimonia to rich citizens' endowing public libraries for the benefit of their fellow citizens. Lucius Flavius, for example, the patron of the city of Dyrrhakhion in modern Albania, gave 170,000 sesterces for the construction of a town library. And a certain Gaius Stertinus Xenophon "dedicated a library to the gods and the people [of Kos] with his own money." Since Gaius was a priest of Asklepios (the god of healing) and Hygieia ("Health") on this island known for its medical school, the library may well have been one specializing in medical texts by Hippokrates and others. We do not have to believe the late story that Hippokrates, upon being appointed librarian in Kos, burnt the out-of-date medical texts, especially since he is said also to have burnt the library along with them.[64]

FIGURE 39
Unopened papyrus roll found alongside a mummy in an Egyptian tomb of ca. 300 B.C. Resin was added as a preservative. Contents unknown, but it would have had some value for the deceased owner, just as the Derveni papyrus (see pp. 46f.) seems to have meant something to its owner. From Thebes, Egypt, ca. 300 B.C. H. 29.2 cm (11 1/2 in.). London, The British Museum, inv. EA 10738.

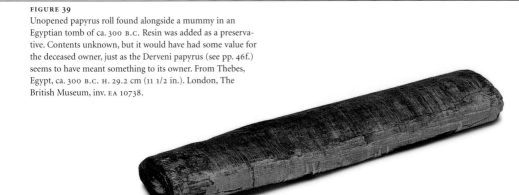

If one could not endow an entire library, one could, then as now, contribute books; in Athens, it was decreed that the more generous donors would have their names engraved on public monuments. More often, though, it was the town that endowed the library out of public funds. By Roman times, Athens was as famous for its libraries as for its racetracks and gymnasia (FIG. 48). If the city were not governed democratically, a monarch could decide to spend his money on a library, as did Ptolemy I Soter (r. 323–283/2 B.C.), the ruler of Alexandria.

Greek monarchs, especially tyrants with something to prove, often acted as patrons of artists, particularly poets. At the very beginning of the bookish Hellenistic age, Ptolemy I institutionalized this practice, freeing such activity from the confines of his own court, and placing it in the more public space of the Mouseion, a name that signified a place to worship the Muses, not in an old-fashioned religious sense, but by gathering the works of literature produced in their honor and then by cataloguing, editing, studying, and emulating them.[65] The Mouseion, in other words, was a combination of a school of the arts, institute for advanced study, and university library, where the librarians were also editors and poets. There were earlier models for this, such as the scheme Theophrastos had in mind when he willed his gardens jointly to ten of his friends and students, so that "they may study and philosophize together" and "regard it as they would a temple."[66] No such temple of learning, though, could compete with Ptolemy's Mouseion in Alexandria. From all over the Greek world he attracted poets, scholars, and scientists; furthermore, he envisioned the Mouseion as what is now called a library of record: All the world's texts were to be gathered together. In the first instance, of course, this would mean the Greek world, but important non-Greek texts were also to be included, in translation, and, given what we know of this library's acquisitiveness, apparently in the original as well.

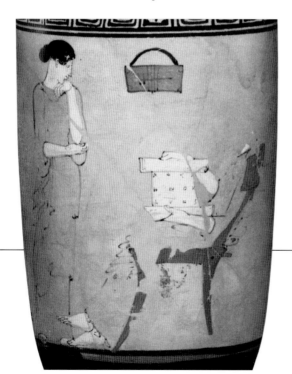

FIGURE 40
Detail of an Athenian vase showing the earliest known scene of one woman reading to another. The artist has arranged the nonsense letters to align vertically, a well-known style (*stoikhedon*) of Attic inscriptions in the mid-fifth century B.C.:

NΔϟT
HNOK
AϟHϟ

Ex Basel market. Photo courtesy of Herbert Cahn.

FIGURE 41
Detail of a late fifth-century-B.C. Athenian vase showing
a woman standing with a papyrus roll in front of another
woman, who is sitting on a rock playing a lyre. Athens,
National Archaeological Museum, inv. 1241.

The first librarian, Demetrios of Phaleron (the port of Athens), was given what every librarian dreams of—unlimited funds to build up a library. When he told Ptolemy (perhaps Ptolemy II Philadelphos, r. 283/2–246 B.C.) that Jewish texts belonged in the library's collection, he was ordered to commission a translation from some of the learned Jews living in Alexandria. That, at any rate, is said to have been the origin of the Septuagint, the Hellenistic Greek translation of the Bible.[67] Perhaps they also collected copies of Egyptian texts.

Even with an unlimited budget, it was not easy to obtain a copy of every Greek book. The Library of Congress and the British Library can demand only those books published in the U.S. and the U.K., respectively. The Ptolemies were known to search for books on all ships docking in Alexandria's harbor. These would be copied and each copy meticulously labeled "from the ships"; the originals were returned to the no-doubt impatient sailors. Less haphazardly, the library sought to borrow important texts held in other cities, most famously the most authentic editions possible of the texts of the tragedians Aiskhylos, Sophokles, and Euripides, which had been deposited in a public archive in order to prevent knowledge of their original words from being lost as directors and actors altered them in subsequent productions.[68] As Galen tells the story, Ptolemy III Euergetes (r. 246–221 B.C.) borrowed the books, giving the Athenians the very handsome sum of fifteen talents (ca. 375 kg) of silver as a deposit; he then had deluxe copies made on the finest papyrus, but he gave the Athenians the copies and kept the originals, forfeiting the deposit. Such was the value placed on acquiring texts in Alexandria.

The men chosen to run the library of Alexandria were poets and scholars. Several are known for the attention they paid to improving the quality of the texts in the library by their careful (or in some cases not so careful) editing and explicating through learned commentaries. Homer, whose texts had been transmitted in wildly different recensions and whose vocabulary contained many obscure words, benefited most from their attention.[69]

The number of volumes in the library of Alexandria at any one time varies markedly from one ancient source to another (forty thousand, or was it seven hundred thousand?), but by the time of Ptolemy III Euergetes very few Greek texts from Homer to his time could have been missing. Too many for any one person to read, said Seneca the Younger (the Roman author of

FIGURE 42
Engraving of a wall-painting showing a woman leaning
against a wall absorbed in her reading, unrolling the text
faster than she rolls it up again. From *Delle antichità di
Ercolano*, vol. 4 (Naples, 1765) 305. Los Angeles, Research
Library, Getty Research Institute.

40

tragedies and philosophical works), who seemed almost glad that the library had burnt in 48 B.C., when Julius Caesar joined forces with Cleopatra and regained Alexandria for her. Our ancient sources are particularly inconsistent on the details, and perhaps not all the books were destroyed. In any case, the library's holdings were restored as much as possible, only to be destroyed once again in A.D. 272, by order of the Roman emperor Aurelian.[70]

Alexandria may have had too many books for any one person to read; all the more reason therefore to catalogue its holdings so that specific volumes could easily be found. This task was taken up not by one of the official librarians but by that most learned of poets, Kallimakhos, who occupied some of his idle hours by compiling lists.[71] Among the many titles ascribed to him, both prose and verse, is the *Pinakes* ("Tables, Lists"); in full, *Lists of Those Eminent in All Areas of Learning, and Their Writings,* which filled 120 book rolls. We have fragmentary remains of fifty-eight of these entries, but many unascribed descriptions of a similar sort in other authors certainly owe their origin to Kallimakhos. The *Pinakes* were arranged first by genre: speeches, laws, history, medicine, philosophy, etc., for prose; epic, lyric, tragedy, comedy, etc., for verse. They were then subdivided alphabetically by author, for each of whom a brief biographical account would precede a summary of his or her writings in the following form: title (if there was one), *incipit* (first words of a text), and length (in number of lines). Further subdivision within genre was made when appropriate. As the fragments show, Kallimakhos also discussed problems of ascription, revision, classification by genre, and literary allusion.

Although, as we have seen, publication of sorts existed in the fifth century B.C., poets wrote for performance. Even when they spoke of immortalizing the object—usually the love object—of their song, they meant that their poems would be recited long into the future. Their frequent invocation of the Muses was an appeal to be able to remember and to perform their compositions. Although poetry was still performed in the Hellenistic age, both in private (especially epigrams) and public (victory hymns, for example), frequent mention is made within poems of writing and of the book that con-

FIGURE 43
Engraving of a wall-painting showing a man seated on a low wall reading a papyrus roll, which he rerolls incorrectly so that the writing is on the exposed side of the roll. From *Delle antichità di Ercolano*, vol. 7 (Naples, 1779) 245. Los Angeles, Research Library, Getty Research Institute.

FIGURE 45

Although it may look as though the student is reading from
the opened scroll, more likely we are to "read" the scene as
one in which the teacher hears the student recite the poem
from memory while the teacher checks his recitation against
the text. In this detail of an Athenian drinking cup from
about 480 B.C., the vase-painter Douris has arranged his
figures to provide maximum information for the viewer,
including the opening words of the poem, which seems to
be an epic about Troy. Berlin, Antikensammlung, inv. F 2285.
Photo: Bildarchiv Preussischer Kulturbesitz/Art Resource, NY.

tains the poem as a physical object. As Peter Bing phrases it, the Muses learn to write.[72]

Three occasional features of Hellenistic poetry demonstrate most clearly the distinction between the poem that is heard and the poem one sees on the page. The first is the poem that is shaped by means of varying line lengths, which combine to give an overall shape to the poem—a shape, furthermore, that illustrates the poem's contents. Six of these so-called *tekhnopaigina* are extant, three by Simias, *Wings, The Axe,* and *The Egg;* and *The Syrinx* (that is, panpipe) ascribed to Theokritos, and two poems entitled *The Altar,* one by Dosiadas, the other by Besantinos.

Besantinos's poem also incorporates the second visual element found in postclassical poetry, the acrostic. Note in FIGURE 49 how the capital first letters of the lines spell out in Greek the words "Olympian, may you offer sacrifices in the course of many years," an appropriate phrase for an altar, which may be addressed to the emperor Hadrian. This then is a relatively late example of the poetic acrostic, but it has been found in Aratos's early second-century-B.C. poem on the heavens, which incorporates the word ΛΕΠΤΗ (*leptos*), "delicate/ refined," both as the first word of line 783 (where it refers to fair weather) and as an acrostic running down the page from 783 to 787. The word *leptos* was used as a key word of Hellenistic aesthetics, making its use here all the more pointed. Kallimakhos and others made a point of praising Aratos's *leptotes,* "refinement," to show that they had recognized the acrostic, although, somewhat surprisingly, it was lost sight of soon afterward and rediscovered only in 1960.[73] Needless to say, an acrostic cannot be detected by the ear. (An acrostic in the first five lines of *Iliad* 24 spelling out *leuke,* "white" is therefore taken to be entirely fortuitous.)

Fortunately, most poets were happy simply to use metaphors drawn from books, producing

FIGURE 46
To the accompaniment of an *aulos* (a double flute), a young
boy recites a poem that ends with the words ΣΤΕΣΙΧΟΡ |
ΟΝ *h*ΥΜΝΟΝ | ΑΓΟΙΣΑΙ, "[Muses?] leading the song
set for the chorus." (See J. D. Beazley, *Corpus Vasorum
Antiquorum, Oxford,* fasc. 1 [Oxford, 1927] 13–14.) Oxford,
Ashmolean Museum, inv. G 138.3.

42

poems that could still be appreciated by the ear. As but one example, consider the following epigram
of Philodemos:

> Thirty-seven years are passing: papyrus columns [*selides*] of my life are now torn off;
> now too, Xanthippe, white hairs begin to show, messengers of the age of intelligence;
> but the harp's voice and revels are still a concern to me, and a fire smolders in my insatiable heart.
> Inscribe Xanthippe immediately as the coronis, Mistress Muses, of this my madness.[74]

The main point of this epigram is that now, at age 37, the narrator (an alternate persona of Philodemos
himself) wishes to put wild parties and revelry behind him and to spend the rest of his life with
Xanthippe. He sees all this, though, in terms of a book: Each year of his life is compared to a text column (*selis*, see p. 30) in a papyrus, which is torn off, much like the movie cliché where days of a calen-
dar fly off into the air to represent the passing of time. And just as a *koronis* is written alongside a *selis*
to mark the end of a significant section of a literary work, so too in the book of life that is Philodemos's
will the Muses inscribe Xanthippe as the outward sign of his new maturity. With this personification of
a coronis, compare an earlier Hellenistic epigram by Meleager, which is narrated by the coronis itself,
announcing that it is the last poem in this particular collection.[75] Philodemos uses the metaphor of the
book of life in his prose as well: "the *paragraphe* of life" (see p. 30), that is, the line marking the end of
a text, a notion borrowed by Horace: *mors ultima linea rerum est,* "death is the last line."[76]

 Philodemos is the author whose prose works were found in greatest number in the Villa dei
Papiri, whose library we can now see in its historical context. Individuals could own books in large
numbers, whether as a necessary adjunct for their own learned or literary activities or as a misleading
public avowal of a learning they do not truly possess. In the second century A.D., Lucian neatly skew-
ered such a person in his *Remarks to an Ignorant Book-buyer,* "Let me tell you that you are choosing
the worst way to attain your object. You think that by buying up all the best books you can lay your
hands on, you will pass for a man of literary tastes: not a bit of it; you are merely exposing thereby
your own ignorance of literature."[77]

 Whereas huge libraries such as the one in Alexandria would need a Kallimakhos to organize its
holdings, an individual could, if he chose, simply arrange his works alphabetically, as Galen the physi-
cian seems to have done, mixing philosophers with medical writers. By the time Romans began to col-

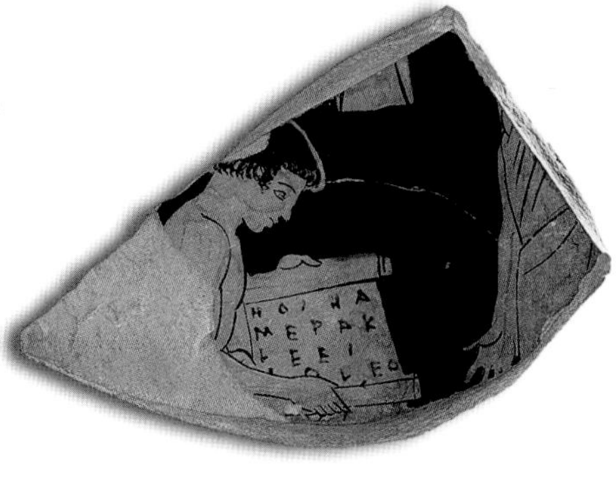

FIGURE 47
Fragment of a vase painted by the Akestorides Painter, ca. 460 B.C. The boy holds a scroll correctly, but the letters are turned 90 degrees; it seems to be a handbook on mythology: *h*οι *h*άλ|μ' Ἑρακ|λέει· | Ἰόλεο(ς), "Those with Herakles: Iolaos," with other names presumably to follow. A wax tablet on the wall and the (partial) male figure at the right suggest that, as with the Douris vase (see FIG. 45), a schoolroom scene is portrayed. Los Angeles, J. Paul Getty Museum, inv. 86.AE.324.

lect Greek works, however, we find frequent references to segregation by language. Thus, Julius Caesar had planned to establish two public libraries in Rome, one for Latin and one for Greek.[78] Cicero had a Latin library distinct from his Greek one. This became so standard among Romans that the immensely rich and vulgar Trimalchio—whose excesses are caricatured by Petronius in his *Satyrica,* and who always has to one-up everybody else—says, "I have three libraries—one Greek and one Latin." That is, Trimalchio first lies about the number of libraries he has and then stupidly starts to enumerate them, only to run out of libraries after the second one.[79]

Almost all the papyri from the Villa dei Papiri were found in one small room in the Villa, which was described by the eighteenth-century excavators as furnished with book cabinets, that is, it was a library (see p. 22; a few rolls were found scattered elsewhere in the building: see FIG. 64). The book rolls that have been read to date are overwhelmingly Greek texts. Given the Roman habit of segregating Roman and Greek libraries, it is thus possible that the still-unexcavated part of the Villa may hold a Latin library. Any Roman work composed before A.D. 79 could be there, including many whose very existence we are ignorant of. What a treat this would be for classical scholars. What could we reasonably hope for? Since the Greek library apparently was Philodemos's own in his day, we can expect to find poems by his Roman friends, whom he addresses in some of his prose works.

Some of those poets are today considered minor, because we know only fragments of their works (e.g., Lucius Varius Rufus, whose didactic poem *On Death* drew on Epicurean themes). The late Roman author Probus names Varius among Vergil's Epicurean associates, and Vergil himself names Varius in his ninth *Eclogue,* where the rustic speaker Lycidas says, "I seem to say nothing worthy of Varius." Even earlier, Vergil had addressed Varius in a witty poem making fun of himself and the problem Roman authors had when trying to adapt Greek themes into the Latin language (*Catalepton* 7). Varius's poem on death would make fascinating reading alongside Lucretius's diatribe on death at the end of his third book of *On the Nature of Things.* It would also help in restoring Philodemos's prose treatise on death (see p. 92).

Philodemos also addresses Publius Quintilius Varus, another of Vergil's Epicurean friends who Servius, the learned commentator on Vergil, said appeared in Vergil's sixth *Eclogue* disguised as the character Mnasylos. Another likely addressee along with Varius and Quintilius in *PHerc.* 253 is Plotius

FIGURE 48
Marble inscription found in the Agora of Athens, on the wall of the Library of Pantainos, which was built ca. A.D. 200: βυβλίον οὐκ ἐξε|νεχθήσεται ἐπεὶ|ὠμόσαμεν· ἀνυγή|σεται ἀπὸ ὥρας πρώ|της μέχρι ἕκτης, "No book shall be removed, since we have sworn thus. Opening hours are from six in the morning until noon." H. 31 cm (12¼ in.). Athens, Agora Excavations, inv. I 2729.

Tucca, who with Varius edited the *Aeneid* for publication after Vergil's death.[80] Most famous of all Philodemos's addressees, however, was Vergil himself, who is named for sure in one Herculaneum papyrus (*PHerc.Paris* 2, one of the papyri taken by Napoleon to France; see p. 55) and very likely also in two others. We have then a group of friends all of whom were poets and, to varying degrees, favorable to Epicurean teachings. Vergil, as we know from yet another *Catalepton* poem, was a student of Siron,[81] who was every bit as famous as Philodemos as a teacher of Epicurean doctrine on the Bay of Naples. Vergil, who spent time there, was sympathetic to the teachings of the Epicureans: "We set sail for a fine port, seeking the learned teachings of great Siron" (*Catalepton* 5.8f.). And in this port of Naples Vergil seems to have inherited Siron's home, according to *Catalepton* 8, which praises in good Epicurean fashion its modest accommodations, just as Philodemos describes his own home in *Epigram* 27[82] (see pp. 83ff.). Siron, as we have seen (p. 6), was mentioned favorably by Philodemos in *PHerc.* 312: It seems clear that Philodemos and Siron were considered part of the extended community of Epicureans living on the Bay of Naples.

What did this company of friends discuss when they met? An easy guess: poetry and Epicurean theory, and, since Philodemos was interested in Epicurean views of literary criticism, how one could inform the other. A more specific answer may be found in one of Horace's poems on the art of poetry, for Horace too may have been, at least occasionally, a member of this circle of friends. Not only does Horace explicitly name Philodemos in one of his *Satires* (1.2), he praises Quintilius Varus for his frank criticism of his (Horace's) poems before they have been published. "Friend," he says, "correct this and correct that." A good and honest man will criticize his friend's dull lines.[83] In every detail of his praise of Quintilius's criticism Horace accepts the precise argument Philodemos makes in his prose work *On Frankness of Speech* about the importance of a friend's offering frank criticism. All Horace does is adapt this from Philodemos's ethical sphere to the aesthetic. Horace's use of two Latin words for "friend" (*sodes* and *amicus*) acknowledges his debt to Philodemos, since friendship is a key Epicurean notion.

Philodemos's personal library of Latin texts, therefore, would reasonably contain the works of Vergil, Horace, Plotius Tucca, Quintilius, and Varius; and these texts constitute a reasonable minimum for what we could expect to find in the Villa's Latin library. Since he never lived in the Villa, Philodemos's own library would presumably have been absorbed into the Roman owner's larger collection, which brings us back to the tantalizing notion that a wealth of literature awaits discovery in

ΒΗΣΑΝΤΙΝΟΥ ΒΩΜΟΣ

Ο λὸς οὔ με λιβρὸς ἱρῶν

Λ ιβάδεσσιν οἷα κάλχης

Υ ποφοινίῃσι τέγγει,

Μ αύλιες δ' ὕπερθε πέτρῃ Ναξίῃ θοούμεναι

5 Π αμάτων φείδοντο Πανός, οὐ στροβίλῳ λιγνύι

Ι ξὸς εὐώδης μελαίνει τρεχνέων με Νυσίων·

Ε ς γὰρ βωμὸν ὁρῇς με μήτε γλούρου

Π λίνθοις μήτ' Ἀλύβης παγέντα βώλοις,

Ο ὐδ' ὃν Κυνθογενὴς ἔτευξε φύτλη

10 Λ αβόντε μηκάδων κέρα,

Λ ισσαῖσιν ἀμφὶ δειράσιν

Ο σσαι νέμονται Κυνθίαις,

Ι σόρροπος πέλοιτό μοι·

Σ ὺν οὐρανοῦ γὰρ ἐκγόνοις

15 Ε ἰνάς μ' ἔτευξε γηγενής,

Τ άων δ' ἀείζωον τέχνην

Ε νευσε πάλμυς ἀφθίτων.

Σ ὺ δ', ὦ πιὼν κρήνηθεν ἥν

Ι νις κόλαψε Γοργόνος,

20 Θ ύοις τ' ἐπισπένδοις τ' ἐμοί

Υ μηττιάδων πολὺ λαροτέρην

Σ πονδὴν ἅδην. ἴθι δὴ θαρσέων

Ε ς ἐμὴν τεῦξιν, καθαρὸς γὰρ ἐγώ

Ι ὸν ἱέντων τεράων οἷα κέκευθ' ἐκεῖνος,

25 Α μφὶ Νέαις Θρηικίαις ὃν σχεδόθεν Μυρίνης

Σ οί, Τριπάτωρ, πορφυρέου φὼρ ἀνέθηκε κριοῦ.

the Villa: poetry (in addition to what we have just talked about and in addition to what has already been found), history (say, now-lost books of Livy), philosophy (Roman Epicureans for a start), tragedy (say, Ennius), comedy (more Terence), technical treatises, private letters, and family archives (which could include letters from Piso's son-in-law Julius Caesar). (See pp. 60–64 and n.116.)

FIGURE 49
The Altar by Besantinos (second century A.D.), printed with bold initial letters to call attention to its acrostic phrase. From A. S. F. Gow, *Bucolici Graeci* (Oxford, 1958) 184. By permission of Oxford University Press.

How to Open and Read
a Charred Papyrus

Imagine the best of circumstances: A papyrus roll has been preserved in a place that is both dry (which in the case of Greek papyri usually means Egypt) and protective of its shape, such as a burial chamber, untouched until opened by responsible archaeologists. The papyrologist merely unrolls the scroll much as any ancient reader would, though probably with a little more care. And if the text had not previously been known, the world is now blessed with a "new" text from antiquity that may be many modern pages in length. Such a perfect scenario is rare. Almost as good is a situation where the papyrus has suffered only minor breakage, so that most of the work is legible, with only a few isolated and unplaceable pieces left over.

Among the major works brought to light in the last century and a half is the *Constitution of Athens* (*Athenaion Politeia*), a work of Aristotle's school containing many important contemporary details about the workings of the Athenian constitution. Notice of its discovery was announced in the London *Times* on 19 January 1891, which delicately described its origin as "a source in Egypt which, for obvious reasons, it is not expedient to specify too particularly"—the chief reason being that it was taken illicitly from a tomb and smuggled past Egyptian customs officials, a practice that did not end in the nineteenth century. The *AthPol,* as classicists usually call it (and pronounce it), was first published in 1891 by F. G. Kenyon, in thirty-six columns, filling seventy-five modern pages with its nearly continous text.[84]

Another author reclaimed from the sands of Egypt is Bakkhylides, a fifth-century-B.C. lyric poet of epinician odes for athletes, who had been praised in antiquity as a worthy second to his contemporary Pindar. From practically nothing, Bakkhylides became a major author. Other discoveries made since then have added significantly to what had been known before: Alkaios, Sappho, Stesikhoros, Simonides, Poseidippos, and Empedokles, to name only poets.

If papyrus is to last outside the dry Egyptian climate, it must be thoroughly dried before decay sets in. Fire does the job nicely, so long as it does no more than carbonize the outer layers. Once carbonized, the papyrus roll must be kept from being crushed into powder. After the Herculaneum papyri, the most noteworthy discovery was that of a carbonized papyrus in a tomb near Derveni, in modern northern Greece, composed perhaps as early as the late fifth century B.C., which makes it our earliest written literary text in Greek. (Earlier writing is found on vases, ostraka, and inscriptions; see FIGS. 20, 23.) The prose text of the Derveni papyrus contains quotations of and commentary on previously unknown hexameter verses ascribed by its author to the mythical poet Orpheus, as well as a quotation from Herakleitos, citing as one continuous passage two sentences that until the discovery of the Derveni papyrus had consistently been cited separately, so that each had it own distinct fragment number (FIG. 50). The text of this papyrus, discovered in 1962, has yet to receive an official publication, as the editors are trying to read the charred and badly broken pieces.[85] Perhaps the spectrographic imaging that will be described below (see pp. 58–59 and FIG. 61) will help them read more of this text.[86]

OPENING CHARRED PAPYRUS ROLLS

The largest hoard of Greek papyrus texts found outside Egypt is that from the Villa dei Papiri. Charred so severely that, when they were found in the eighteenth century, they were at first taken to be pieces of wood and occasionally burnt for fuel, they were and still are, so difficult to open and read that many rolls remain closed carbon blocks. Many that have been opened are only now, two and a half centuries after their discovery, revealing their text to the latest viewing techniques (FIG. 51).

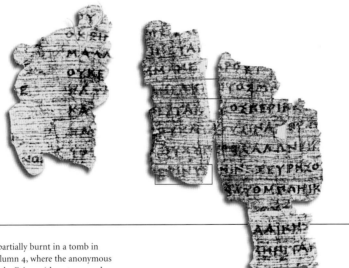

FIGURE 50
The Derveni papyrus, found partially burnt in a tomb in northern Greece. Shown is column 4, where the anonymous author quotes Herakleitos on the Erinyes (these two words are outlined), the Furies who will punish the sun if it fails to observe its natural limits. Photo courtesy of Kyriakos Tsantsanoglou. Shown actual size.

FIGURE 51
One of the many still-unopened papyrus rolls from the Villa
dei Papiri, now kept in the Officina dei Papiri in Naples.
Photo: Sandra Sider.

48

Paderni had simply and crudely knifed some rolls in half vertically, an action guaranteed to destroy letters on each line crossing the cut (FIG. 52). Then, to make matters worse, he had scooped out the center of the roll, where the scroll, because of its narrow diameter, would offer him only the smallest strips of text; that is, he destroyed the parts he felt would be least likely to excite interest from his patrons and important visitors. He kept scraping away until he got to a suitably impressive passage of Greek text. This is all the more unfortunate because the center of the roll suffered least from the heat, mud, and water of the volcanic eruption. The center, that is, could have been unrolled much like an undamaged papyrus from Egypt, even if more slowly and carefully. Moreover, since the very center of

the roll contained the end of the text (see p. 30), it also contained information about author, title, book number, and perhaps stichometric data (listing the number of lines) that would help the modern editor. A few papyri from the Villa (*De Musica* and some of the books *On Vices*) also have this information at the beginning of the text, but, as we have said, the beginnings of the rolls suffered the most damage, so that most of these are lost to us.

After Paderni's largely crude and ruinous attempts to unroll the papyri, other techniques were tried. King Charles invited Raimondo di Sangro, prince of Sansevero, to the Royal Palace in Portici.[87] Di Sangro thought that mercury, with its slippery ability to fall between cracks, would help to separate the charred layers of the papyri. Mercury, though, while liquid in appearance, is also quite dense. Pouring it down the edges of the rolls did nothing but crumble and destroy whatever it touched. Undeterred, di Sangro thought that complete immersion in mercury, providing pressure from all sides would do better. More rolls were destroyed.

The next suggestion was to use rose water; this, too, proved to be a disaster, but at least the destroyed rolls smelled better than they had before.

A chemist, Gaetano la Pira, tried a noisome "vegetable gas," another failure, as we read in a contemporary description: "The greatest part of each mass flew, under this trial, into useless atoms; besides, not a character was to be discovered upon any single piece. The dreadful odor drove us all from the Museum. This, in fact, is a part of the royal palace, which, if the court had been there, must,

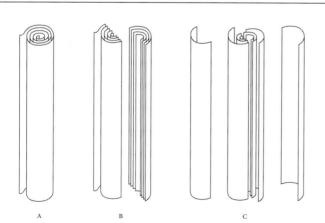

FIGURE 52
Obtaining *scorze:* (A) Unopened roll; (B) the roll cut down the middle, which always destroys some letters; (C) the *scorze* being separated. Drawing: Marian Stewart.

A   B   C

also, have been precipitately abandoned."[88]

In 1753 King Charles turned for help to the head of the Vatican Library, who sent him Father Antonio Piaggio (FIG. 53), whose harsh criticisms of Paderni we have already heard of (see pp. 22f.). The serious business of patient unrolling now began. When Piaggio saw Paderni's method—cutting the papyri in half lengthwise—he reacted with horror.[89] Fortunately, Paderni later realized that these vertical cuts need not be complete. Two cuts opposite each other could stop short of the center—now called the *midollo*, or "marrow," as though the roll were bone.[90] The original roll was now divided into three: the *midollo* and two half-cylinders (FIG. 54). Since a papyrus was rolled with its blank surface facing out, at this point the inner, concave, surface of each half-cylinder could be read immediately, assuming of course some minimal legibility. Although these half-cylinders surrounded the "marrow," with a mixing of metaphors, each outer piece came to be called *scorza* ("bark" or "husk"); this word was applied also to the entire half-cylinder comprising the individual sheets. In the process of "husking," *scorzatura*, where each layer was destroyed as it was removed from the center out, only the last layer could be preserved, usually by gluing it to a thin animal membrane.[91] As David Blank kindly informs me, "these 'last leaves' normally contain at least fragments of various layers, and in most cases these layers have in part peeled off from the preserved piece, exposing glimpses of layers further toward the exterior."[92]

When papyrus rolls from Egypt are opened, the sheets can be placed between protective glass or stored in shallow drawers, and then left for decades before a papyrologist sits down to read them. With the Herculaneum papyri, on the other hand, opening and reading had to go hand in hand. Because of the destructive nature of *scorzatura*, careful transcription of the letters and, even better, precise drawings (called by the Italian word *disegni*) of all marks that could be letters were made before unpeeling the next layer. Often each layer could be separated without too much loss. A frequent occurrence, however, was that small parts of the first, inmost, layer stuck to the one below it. (Since to the viewer the inmost layer was above the next one, the former came to be called *sovrapposto*, the latter *sottoposto*.) There was now the real danger that a bit of the *sovrapposto* came to be read and transcribed as though it belonged to its *sottoposto*.

FIGURE 54
Here two cuts are made in a papyrus roll; the cuts stop before they meet in the center of the roll, allowing an undamaged *midollo* (the center of the roll, which contains the end of the text) to be unrolled. Drawing: Marian Stewart.

In order to facilitate separation of the layers, each vertical half-cylinder was occasionally cut into two, a top and a bottom, of course with further loss of letters at the break. Some few rolls were broken into three—top, middle, and bottom. In addition, because the pieces were often set aside or even separated before being inventoried, it was common for the pieces—*midollo* and however many cylindrical pieces—each to be given a separate *PHerc.* number; more numbers could be assigned, depending on how the roll was broken up. Later scholars have to apply many sorts of tests—measuring the height of the papyri, looking for similar arguments and phrases, checking the eighteenth-century archives, etc.—in order to determine which number goes with which.[93] (See the numbers in FIG. 66.)

The *midollo,* as we have seen, was not too charred, so it could be unrolled without (major) breakage, but it still lacked the flexibility of a new or unscorched roll. It was for these *midolli* that Piaggio invented an ingenious device (FIG. 55). Animal membrane was attached to the outer edge of a papyrus roll; ribbons or strings were attached to the membrane, and the former were in turn tied to a bar set above the *midollo,* which by the force of its own weight was allowed to pull away from the skin, that is, slowly unroll. How slowly we learn from an anonymous contemporary account "from a learned Gentleman of Naples."[94]

> It is incredible to imagine what this man ["father Antonio, a writer at the Vatican"] contrived and executed. He made a machine, with which (by the means of certain threads, which being gummed, stuck to the back part of the papyrus, where there was no writing), he begins, by degrees, to pull, while with a sort of ingraver's instrument he loosens one leaf from the other (which is the most difficult part of all), and then makes a sort of lining to the back of the papyrus, with exceeding thin leaves of onion [before he changed to animal membranes] (if I mistake not), and with some spirituous liquor, with which he wets the papyrus, by little and little he unfolds it. All this labor cannot be well comprehended without seeing. With patience superior to what a man can imagine, this good father has unrolled a pretty large piece of papyrus, the worst preserved, by way of trial. . . . After he has loosened a piece, [he] takes it off where there are no letters; and places it between two crystals[95] for the better observation; and then, having an admirable talent in imitating characters, he copies it with all the lacunae, which are very numerous in this scorched papyrus. . . . The worst is, the work takes up so much time, that a small quantity of writing requires five or six days to unroll, so that a whole year is already consumed about half this roll.

FIGURE 55
Schematic drawing of one of Antonio Piaggio's machines
for unrolling papyrus rolls, designed to apply tension to
the edge of a roll. About 2.5 cm (1 in.) could be unrolled
per day. The text illustrated is one of the machine's first
successes, ΦΙΛΟΔΗΜΟΥ ΠΕΡΙ ΜΟΥϹΙΚΗϹ,
Philodemos *On Music*. From Giacomo Castrucci, *Tesoro
letterario di Ercolano* (Naples, 1852), pl. IV, p. 10. Los Angeles,
Research Library, Getty Research Institute.

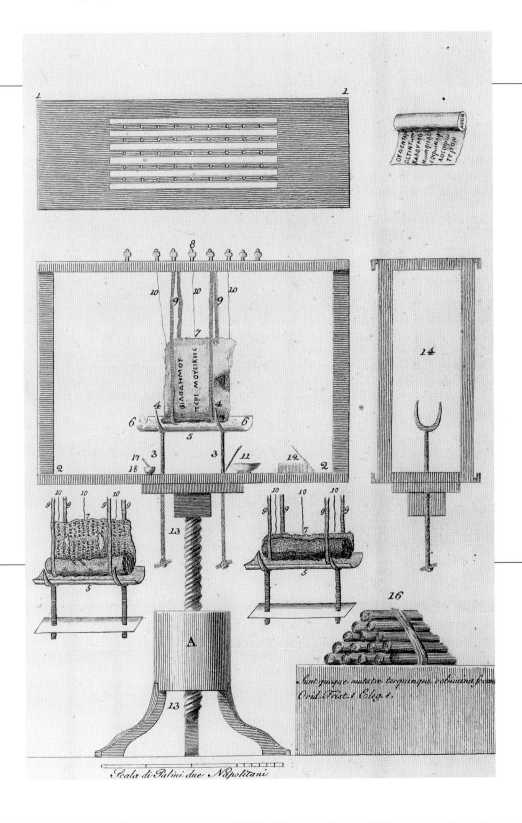

Fortunately, Piaggio had the patience to wait out the process, as well as the fortitude to stand up to Paderni's attempt to keep him from working on the papyri because of his lack of speed. "You must intend to camp out here for many years, if you proceed with such great delicacy to uncover a little bit and take so much time; you must peel [*scorzare*], you must peel; if not, you are insuring that you will never accomplish anything."[96] The first works opened by Piaggio's machine were Philodemos's *On Music* 4 (*PHerc.* 1497), *Rhetoric* 2 (*PHerc.* 1672 and 1674), and *On Vices and Their Corresponding Virtues* (*PHerc.* 1675).[97]

A papyrus found in Egypt can be kept in one piece; after transcription and photographing, it can simply be rerolled. The Herculaneum papyri are far more brittle, but they too could be rerolled, as in fact was done by Piaggio's first machine. Later models, however, called for cutting the papyrus as an opened stretch reached the top of the machine. Hence, every so often in the unrolling a cut would be made—this time carefully between columns of text—and the papyrus fastened by pins or glue to a stiff board. Another contrast: Papyrus sheets and pieces found in Egypt are usually placed between two sheets of glass that are then taped together, allowing the papyrus to be handled and read without further physical contact. Those from Herculaneum, however, are too brittle; if placed between glass, they would be crushed almost to powder. The papyri can be delicately fastened to a board, but they cannot be put between glass (see illustration on back cover). Instead, they are stored in shallow drawers.

Essentially this same system of glue and skin was occasionally used by Piaggio to separate outer layers of *scorze* from those to which they were attached. That is, he worked this time in a direction opposite that of the method described above, in which *sovrapposto* was removed (and usually destroyed) from *sottoposto*.

This method had the clear advantage of preserving each of the layers, but it led to a subsequent confusion that has only recently been sorted out. Piaggio kept careful records of the papyri he opened, identifying them by numbers; later, while inventorying them after Paderni's death, he assigned new numbers, which they still have. What had been lost to later scholars, therefore, was the order in which *scorze* were opened. Let's look again at the *scorzatura* method described above, in which layers were read from the inside out. The first layer was labeled "1," the second "2," and so on. Likewise, in going from the outer layers inward, the pieces were labeled 1, 2, 3, etc., in the order in which they were first detached. In time, *all* the edited papyri were read in this assigned numerical order. Numbering from the *midollo* outward, however, led to *reading* the edited text in this order, which is the reverse order of how some works (like *On Music* and *On Piety*) were originally ordered. It might be argued that James Joyce's *Finnegans Wake* would or should not lose any of its quality by being read page by page in reverse order, but the same cannot be said of Philodemos. Nonetheless, once this error had been established, scholars proceeded to read some of his texts in precisely this way. That they could claim to be able to trace the run of Philodemos's argument even when it was read backward attests to their great philological skills, as well as to their powers of self-deception. Fortunately, even if only relatively recently, two observant scholars working independently of each other realized that this was the case: Dirk Obbink while editing *On Piety* and Daniel Delattre while editing *On Music*. As a result, this reordering and rereading of the columns in many previously edited Herculaneum papyri has come to be known as the Obbink-Delattre method.[98]

The world's first publication of a Herculaneum papyrus occurred in 1793, with *Herculanensium Voluminum quae supersunt,* the first series dedicated to these papyri, with Philodemos's *On Music* 4, edited by Carlo Maria Rosini (FIGS. 56, 57). (On the publishing history of the papyri, see appendix 2.)

After Piaggio died in 1796, work on the papyri slowed down, and then had to cease completely during the political turmoil of those years. King Ferdinand IV of Naples (and III of Sicily) and his wife Maria Carolina (daughter of Empress Maria Theresa of Austria) had done much to make Naples powerful and cultured, but, in opposing the overthrow of the monarchy in France, they sadly underestimated Napoleon's power and ambition. Although at peace with France since 1796, they hoped to take advantage of Napoleon's expedition in Egypt. Encouraged by his wife, and with the help of British Rear Admiral Lord Nelson, Ferdinand invaded Rome, but could not hold it for long.[99] Nor could the royal household remain any longer in Naples. In late 1798, work on the papyri was suspended as Ferdinand and Maria Carolina, fleeing Napoleon's invading forces with their entire court, sailed to Palermo in Sicily onboard one of Nelson's ships, taking with them all the papyri, which had been packed in sawdust.

The French arrived early the next year, when they helped Naples's republican class establish the short-lived Reppublica Partenopea, in memory of the land's early Greek name (see p. 2). The republicans, however, were unable to make a success of their new government. Ferdinand soon regained power and, having already sent back the papyri, still cushioned by sawdust in their original packing crates, he was able in 1802 to recall his court to Naples. In 1806 the court again fled to Palermo, ahead

Philodemos *On Music* Book 4, the first of the Herculaneum texts to be published, in 1793. Illustrated is the volume's presentation of column 16, with an engraving of the drawing (*disegno*) of the text facing a transcription of the Greek and a Latin translation in parallel columns. Supplements where the text has lacunae are printed in red. The sentence on lines 16–21 reads, "Scenes in Homer have made it quite clear that music is a natural part of the symposium." From *Herculanensium Voluminum quae supersunt,* vol. 1 (Naples, 1793), col. XVI, pp. 70–71. Los Angeles, Research Library, Getty Research Institute.

of Napoleon's invading army. This time, though, the papyri stayed put in the Royal Museum in Portici, almost directly above the ancient town of Herculaneum (FIG. 58).

The next, but not the last, clergyman to play an important role in reading the papyri was the British Reverend John Hayter (1756–1818), who, in 1800 at the instigation of the Prince of Wales (later King George IV of England), was invited to Naples to aid in the unrolling and editing of the rolls.[100] With the prince taking care of his expenses, Hayter supervised and directed the work of the Officina dei Papiri, as it was then and still is called. In the four years between 1802 and 1806, he oversaw the unrolling of about two hundred rolls. He also supervised the careful transcription of about half of them. Engravings were made from the *disegni* (literally, drawings, i.e., transcriptions) for use in eventual publication of the texts. Because the *disegni* were made soon after the papyri were opened, before they suffered any further damage, they represent important evidence for later editors. Often, given the destructive nature of the *scorzatura* method, these *disegni* are all that is left. They thus now constitute primary witnesses for the original texts, much as a medieval parchment manuscript of, say, Euripides, although many centuries later than the fifth-century-B.C. original, is now considered a primary witness.

The *disegni* that were taken to England (see below) and those now in Naples, labeled *O* [Oxford] and *N* [Naples], respectively, must always be cited in printed editions. It is fortunate, then, that great care was taken in preparing these drawings. Men who were themselves ignorant of Greek were given the task of carefully copying by hand the columns of text as they were unrolled (and then often cut into manageable sections).[101] Not knowing Greek, the draftsmen had no preconceived idea of what letter a squig-

gle might be; they simply followed what was for them pure shape. Afterwards, the transcriptions were examined by people who did know Greek, members of the Accademia Ercolanese (one of them being Hayter), and errors were corrected before the text was engraved and published (FIG. 59; see also FIG. 67).[102] To motivate the men in his employ, Hayter offered in addition to their regular salary a bonus of one *carlino* (a small coin struck by the Bourbon monarchs) for each successfully transcribed line. Hayter wrote in his *Report*, "Such an arrangement of pay was not ill calculated to secure the most attentive diligence, and most attentive carefulness, both in the unfolder, and in the transcriber. . . . In a word, he who unfolded, and he who copied, while each, for his own sake, took all possible pains, most advantageously checked, and animated each other" (p. 53).

Napoleon was not one to accept losses willingly; by 1806, with Ferdinand again in exile, Naples was put under the kingship of Napoleon's brother Joseph.[103] Hayter at first accompanied the court to Palermo, along with the *disegni,* whose transference to engravings he supervised. In 1809 he returned to England. Sir William Drummond, the British minister to Naples from 1806 to 1809, took the *disegni* with him on his return to England since he, but not the Neapolitans, assumed the *disegni* and those engravings made in Palermo to be the property of the English crown. He also took *disegni* made before Hayter's arrival, to which obviously the English crown had no claim.[104]

Further attempts to open and read the papyri given to, or taken by, Napoleon were made in France in the summer of 1803. A committee was formed to tackle the problem, but since it comprised a mathematician, a philologist, an encyclopedist, an art historian, and an archaeologist, it is not surprising that they were unable to improve upon Piaggio's machine, an example of which had been brought to Paris.

The greater number of rolls that arrived in England—six in 1802 and fourteen more in 1816—were put in the hands of scientists, who tried variations on the gases and liquids used earlier in Italy.[105] A physicist, Thomas Young, successfully separated some rolls by exposing them to air so moist that it lent some flexibility to the brittle papyrus. He also, unfortunately, tried immersing some rolls in water, which, if nothing else, washed away the water-soluble ink.[106] The president of the Royal Society, Sir Joseph Banks, built an unrolling machine based on a diagram sent from Naples. He too tried to soften the papyri, but his variation of the earlier Italian experiment with mercury produced equally destructive results. Other machines were built. When the second batch of rolls arrived in England in 1816, the famous chemist Humphry Davy was invited to try his hand on them. His first attempt was not chemical; he simply tried to hasten the unrolling process by pulling on a piece of linen that had been (as in Piaggio's original) glued to the papyrus. This extra pressure, however, often removed more than one layer at a time.[107]

Davy then went to Naples in 1819, where more rolls were available for the experiments he had in mind. One called for warming a papyrus roll that had been placed within a glass tube that itself was surrounded by a copper tube; here again, although the papyrus separated, it was not always into single layers. Davy also tried smoking rolls with sulfur gas in order to make them more supple before they were attached to Piaggio's machine; again, the papyrus separated only into multiple layers. Adding iodine chlorine solution to the sulfur did not help. Other chemical agents did actual damage, if not to the structure of the papyrus, then by dissolving the letters. Davy gave up and left Naples. Once again, the papyri were opened by Piaggio's machine alone. Some decades later, further attempts were made

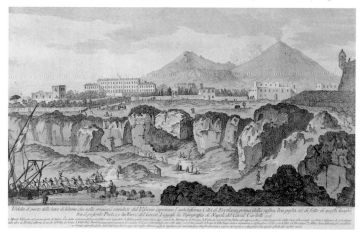

FIGURE 58
Engraving of the Royal Palace in Portici at the foot of Mt. Vesuvius, 1765–1779. The papyrus rolls were kept and studied at the palace in the first decades after their discovery. From Filippo Morghen, *Vedute nel regno Napoli* (Naples, ca. 1780), pl. 2. Los Angeles, Research Library, Getty Research Institute.

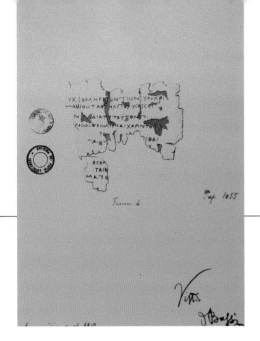

FIGURE 59
One of the original pencil drawings (*disegni*) made of a *scorza* of *PHerc.* 1055, "framm. [fragment] 4," from an unknown work of Demetrios Lakon. Below is the approval ("Visto" = seen) given to the drawing by Domenico Bassi. Photo: Sandra Sider.

to apply chemicals. These too failed.

Nothing new was tried until well into the twentieth century, when Anton Fackelmann, a librarian in Vienna who had had some success with carbonized papyri in his own collection and with the carbonized Derveni papyrus (see pp. 46f.), was invited to apply his techniques in Naples in 1965.[108] Of the more than twelve hundred fragments he examined, he thought only those with the least amount of charring could be opened. To the mechanical, chemical, and caloric techniques attempted earlier, Fackelmann added that of electromagnetism. With a heat lamp held under a thick pane of glass on which the papyrus was supported, he managed to create positive and negative electromagnetic fields between the layers that gently pushed them apart, much as two magnets aligned with opposite poles facing each other will repel each other. This was ingenious enough, but Fackelmann also had the idea of coating the now-separated papyri with a natural transparent resin that would not only strengthen the papyrus's fabric, but also lend it some elasticity. (His idea to place the now-opened papyrus in hermetically sealed glass was not adopted, as this made it harder to make out the letters.) Another clever part of what soon came to be called the Fackelmann method was to increase the flexibility of the sheets with juice obtained from living papyrus plants, which would seem to be the most natural liquid for the dried papyrus cells to absorb.

READING CHARRED PAPYRI

Up to this point we have surveyed the various ways devised to open the rolls; that is, to expose their writings so they can be read. In many cases, the interior columns have proved to be fairly legible and, as already mentioned, they were transcribed immediately or not long after opening. The closer the

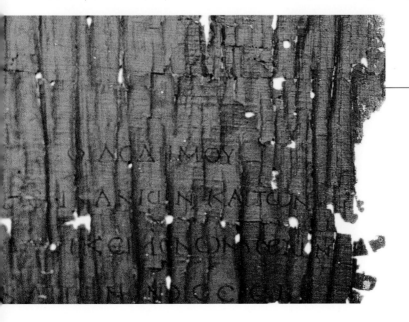

FIGURE 60
A charred Philodemos papyrus seen in ordinary light. ΦΙΛΟΔΗΜΟΥ ("by Philodemos") is legible on the first line. Photo: Sandra Sider.

FIGURE 61

PHerc. 1491, cornice 4, viewed in natural light (*right*), this roll was long thought to be in Latin. Only with multispectral imaging (*left*) was it seen, quite clearly, that the text is Greek. © 2002 Biblioteca Nazionale "Vittorio Emanuele III" di Napoli and the Institute for the Study and Preservation of Ancient Religious Texts (ISPART) at Brigham Young University, Provo, UT. All rights reserved. Digital photograph by Gianluca Del Mastro with permission of BNN Officina dei Papiri "Marcello Gigante." Reproduced by permission of the Ministero per i Beni e le Attività Culturali.

columns were to the outer surface of the roll, however, the darker and hence more illegible they were. Many of these sheets are grey, not much lighter than the letters they contain. They look, in fact, like a black-and-white photograph taken at dusk with the wrong camera settings. Imagine trying to read a newspaper by starlight on a moonless night (FIG. 60). Other sheets had lost much of their surface to moisture and imperfect separation. In sum, many of the columns could be read only partially or not at all. All that could be done until recently was to put the text under increasingly sophisticated microscopes. Binocular microscopes, for example, provide a three-dimensional image that helps the viewer more easily to distinguish between ink and other dark marks, including dark fibers.

In the early 1970s a group of Norwegian papyrologists were working on ways to separate the layers of papyri that had been pasted together to make mummy cartonnage by means of a gelatinous glue that could later be removed with acetic acid without harm to the papyri. Led by Knut Kleve, this group came to Naples and began a long and fruitful collaboration with the Officina dei Papiri. Their technological advances have benefited all subsequent papyrologists. What set them apart from their predecessors was their application of computers.

In essence, the Norwegians developed a pattern-recognition program that, when given a carefully rendered drawing made from a microphotograph of an incomplete letter, which was often in several separate segments, would suggest one or more possible complete letters. This is roughly comparable to the FBI's fingerprint recognition program. One major difference between the two is that, whereas there is only one match possible for a partial fingerprint, there is a fairly wide range of possible forms for each Greek letter. Although one could argue that this is nothing more than

FIGURE 62

A computer program isolates individual letters and exaggerates by means of artificial colors the boundaries between letters and background. Photo: IBM. Reproduced by courtesy of Mario Capasso.

what skilled papyrologists have always done, there is no doubt that this new technique of "letteralogy" (as they somewhat inelegantly termed it) is at the very least a valuable adjunct to the microscope (see FIG. 69).[109]

Microscopes and recognition programs help the naked eye make sense of what it sees. There are, however, papyrus sheets so darkened that to the naked eye the very presence of writing is impossible to discern. The human eye cannot separate the black of the letters from the black of the surrounding page. Astronomers trying to see the dimmest stars at the farthest reaches of the cosmos have faced the same problem. Able to tap funds far in excess of those available to philologists, astronomers have been able to develop techniques of multispectral imaging. Beyond the visible spectrum a star will emit electromagnetic waves different from those of the surrounding space, a difference that can be captured and manipulated by computers attached to telescopes until dim is separated from dimmer on the screen and the contrast is perfectly clear to the eye. Eventually, these same techniques were applied to burnt papyri, as well as to highly faded works of art (FIG. 61).[110] This process can also detect letters otherwise too dim to see because of water damage during the eruption.

Infrared and ultraviolet lights have long been used to bring out text and images no longer visible to the naked eye (FIG. 62). Such lights have been particularly useful for reading palimpsests—manuscripts (usually on parchment) that have been written on again after the previous text had been erased.[111] The overlapping images can be adjusted to increase the contrast on the monitor, at which point the image of sharpest contrast is stored in the computer's memory, from which hard copies can be produced.[112] Even with all this sensitive visualization, the naked eye must still be used; if nothing else, there is still the problem that *sovraposti* and *sottoposti* may not have been entirely separated, with the result that letters from one layer may be thought to belong with those of another. The papyrologist can detect this by moving the papyri back and forth in the glancing natural light of the Officina dei Papiri; the two-dimensional computer image cannot distinguish between layers.

The Books in
the Villa dei Papiri

Introduction

As Camillo Paderni first reported (see p. 20), the majority of the books found in Herculaneum are philosophical treatises; of these, the majority are Epicurean; and of these again, the majority are not by Epikouros himself, but by one of his followers, Philodemos, about whom almost nothing was known before the recovery of the Villa's library.[113] After the initial announcement of a rediscovered library in a Roman villa from the first centuries B.C. and A.D., it was widely hoped that such valuable literary and historical texts as a contemporary manuscript of Vergil or the lost books of Livy would soon be found. People were therefore not happy to learn instead of the library's actual nature: mainly Greek philosophical texts. Epikouros may have been the primary philosophical inspiration for Lucretius's great Latin epic *On the Nature of Things (De rerum natura),* but he himself was long considered the founder of a school important more for historical reasons than for philosophical ones. In the 1880s, Comparetti summed it up:

> If we consider the expectation aroused and long maintained by the discovery of the Herculaneum papyri, and calculate how much scholars have recovered in the three main publications to date, . . . then it is undeniable that all in all the impression produced is one of sadness and disappointment. What has been gained is in inverse proportion to what was hoped for. It seemed that what were mainly expected were Latin texts, which, written in the most felicitous period of Latin letters, would all certainly have been of great importance. Instead, the Latin works not only constitute the smallest minority, but those few that have been found are reduced to a few fragments almost all of which are illegible. It was hoped that the Greek texts would be historical or poetical; instead we now possess only philosophical texts. Even these could have been important ones, but what was desired were lost works from the main philosophical schools, since our direct knowledge of the great Greek philosophical schools is limited to Plato's Academy and Aristotle's Lyceum.[114]

Where do the papyri fall short, then? In not giving us enough Epikouros in anything more than small fragments (although we now know far more of him from the papyri than Comparetti was aware of), and, when they do prove to be more complete and legible, they are the works not of Epikouros but

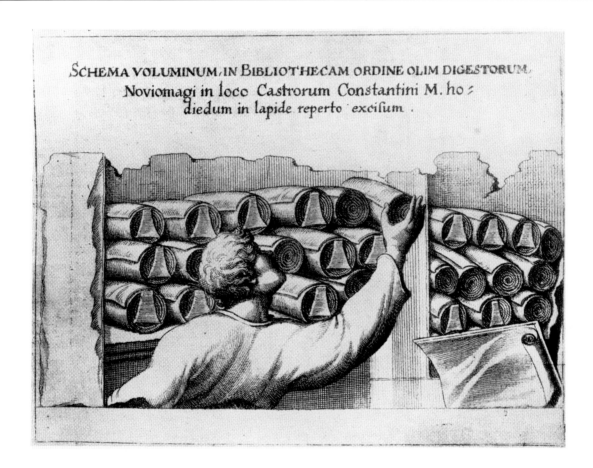

FIGURE 63

Book rolls lying on shelves so that the identifying *sillybos*
for each hangs down over the edge of the roll. Drawing of
a now-lost relief on a Roman funerary monument from
Neumagen, Germany, second half of second century A.D.
From Wilhelm von Massow, *Die Grabmäler von Neumagen*
(Berlin, 1932), fig. 141, p. 243.

FIGURE 64
Findspots of the papyri in the Villa. Before the eruption, the
papyri were stored in *capsae* (see FIG. 31) and on shelves and
consulted on nearby tables. It appears that attempts to remove
the papyri during the eruption were abandoned. The blank
spot on the plan to the top and right of the open courtyard
represents unexcavated rooms, some of which could contain
more papyrus rolls. Cf. FIG. 6. Drawing by Marian Stewart.

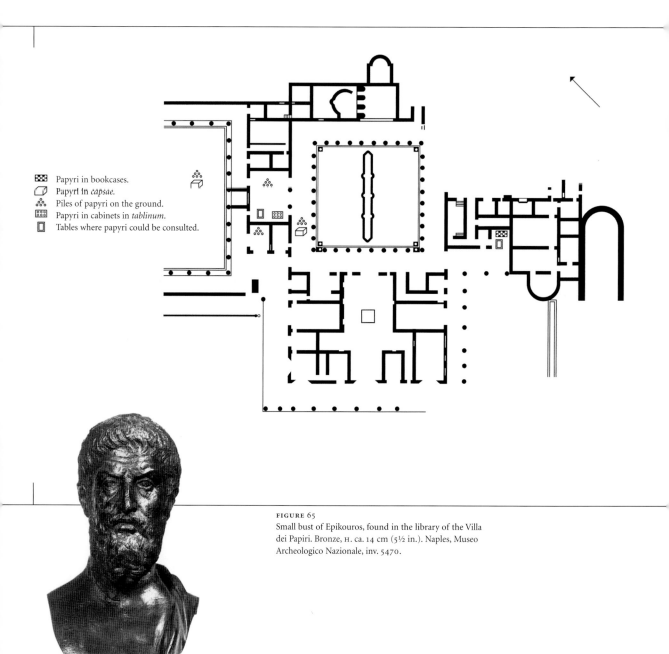

☒ Papyri in bookcases.
▱ Papyri in *capsae*.
⋰ Piles of papyri on the ground.
▦ Papyri in cabinets in *tablinum*.
▯ Tables where papyri could be consulted.

FIGURE 65
Small bust of Epikouros, found in the library of the Villa
dei Papiri. Bronze, H. ca. 14 cm (5½ in.). Naples, Museo
Archeologico Nazionale, inv. 5470.

of Philodemos, "an obscure verbose, inauthentic Epicurean from Cicero's time."

Talk about ingratitude. If nothing else, Philodemos was so faithful an Epicurean that even if nothing of Epikouros had been found, we would still know more about him than before. Let us grant that Philodemos would not be high up, let alone first, on anyone's list of texts to be restored if given a choice. We have already mentioned Vergil and Livy. Comparetti wanted more of Philodemos's poetry, which, truth to tell, is more fun than his prose. Norman Douglas, in his still delightful book on Naples and vicinity, *Siren Land* (1911), even went so far as to hope that some day the "lava of Herculaneum" would reveal the memoirs of the emperor Tiberius, who spent much time on Douglas's beloved island of Capri, "as well as the lost historical works of Pliny the Elder,[115] Cremutius Corda, Paterculus, Seneca, and others"—a list that contains some rather odd choices. William Wordsworth, not surprisingly, wanted more poetry:

> O ye who patiently explore
> The wreck of Herculanean lore
>   What rapture, could you seize
> Some Theban fragment, or unroll
> One precious tender-hearted scroll
>   Of pure Simonides.[116]

Later, we shall see more precisely how valuable Philodemos's treatises are. For now, let us simply attempt a catalogue of the Villa's library. Or libraries: The Latin books may have been housed apart from the Greek ones (see p. 43). Although most of the philosophical texts—over eight hundred—were found on the shelves and floor of one small room, another room, the *tablinum* (roughly, living room), which was often used for the storage of books or family archives,

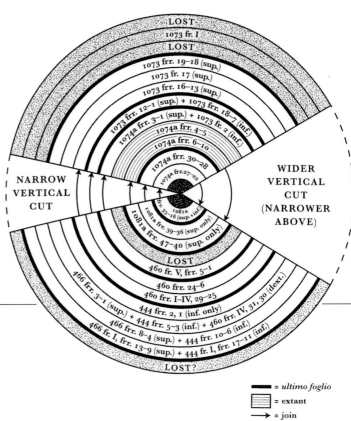

FIGURE 66
Richard Janko's reconstruction of a cross-section of the roll containing Philodemos *On Poems* Book 1 (not to scale). Note how much was lost because of the cuts made to separate the roll into two. "Sup." means that only the upper half of the roll is preserved, "inf." only the lower. See Richard Janko, *Philodemus: On Poems Book 1* (Oxford, 2000), fig. 2, p. 105. By permission of Oxford University Press.

contained a wooden case with rolls piled up on the shelves (FIG. 63). Some of the Latin papyri were found here (FIG. 64). About a hundred other papyri were found in wooden boxes outside another room, which suggests that there may have been an attempt to remove the papyri during the eruption.[117] The small room with the largest number of books (and a bust of Epikouros, FIG. 65) may have been only part of the Greek library originally in the Villa. Where, for example, is Plato and Aristotle, to say nothing of Homer, Sappho, and Euripides, to name only some of the authors cited by Philodemos himself in the course of his literary treatises?[118] Where are his own epigrams? Piso's heirs may have decided to divide up the Greek books on the basis of what they valued versus those they thought little of. Plato and the poets in one room, the (as they might view it) boring Epicureans in another. For the sake of simplicity, however, we shall continue to refer collectively to all the books found in the Villa as the (one) library.

How many volumes have been found? This is not easy to determine accurately. It is clear that a number of rolls were discarded in the early 1750s, before they were recognized as papyri. Quite a few rolls were destroyed during attempts to unroll them. Some rolls are still fused together in clumps; others have been cut in two for the purpose of getting to the texts, each half of the one original roll receiving a separate inventory number; still other rolls have suffered further breakage, again with each chunk numbered separately. Thus, Richard Janko edited the first book of Philodemos's *On Poems* from pieces (each containing many separated sheets of broken papyri) given six different *PHerc.* numbers (FIG. 66). Some rolls, although separate and unbroken, have yet to be opened. Still, scholars have been far from idle in identifying and deciphering hundreds of rolls; they estimate the number of complete rolls represented by the fragments to have been close to eleven hundred (see also p. 73). The following pages offer a selective census of the Herculaneum papyri, drawn from the very useful *Catalogo dei Papiri Ercolanesi*, a description and full bibliography of each papyus,[119] as well as from recent issues of *Cronache Ercolanesi*, where most new discoveries are discussed in detail.

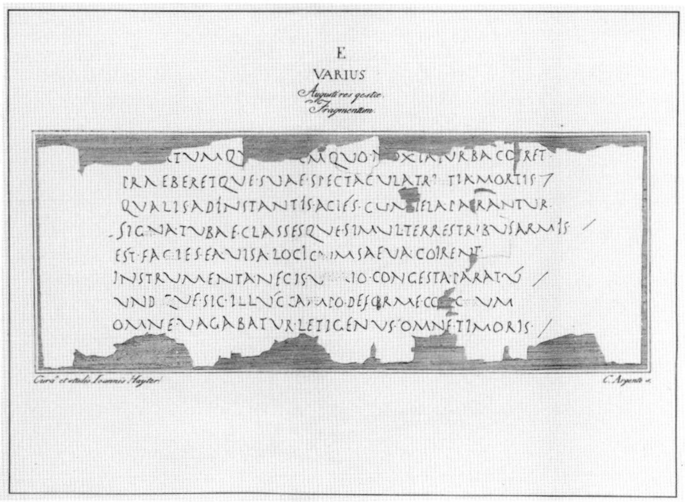

FIGURE 67
Column 5 of the *Carmen de Bello Actiaco* (here called *Augusti Res Gestæ*, "The Accomplishments of Augustus [Caesar]"), transcribed on page 67. Engraving made from a *disegno* supervised by John Hayter, who, as the heading shows, thought that the author of this Latin poem was Varius. From Walter Scott, *Fragmenta Herculanensia* (Oxford, 1885), pl. E.

FIGURE 68
Selected Latin scripts found in Herculaneum in the texts of Ennius, Lucretius, *Carmen de Bello Actiaco,* and an anonymous prose text (*PHerc.* 1475). Drawing by Marian Stewart, based on Knut Kleve, "An Approach to the Latin Papyri from Herculaneum," in *Storia Poesia e Pensiero nel mondo antico* (Naples, 1994), pl. 316.

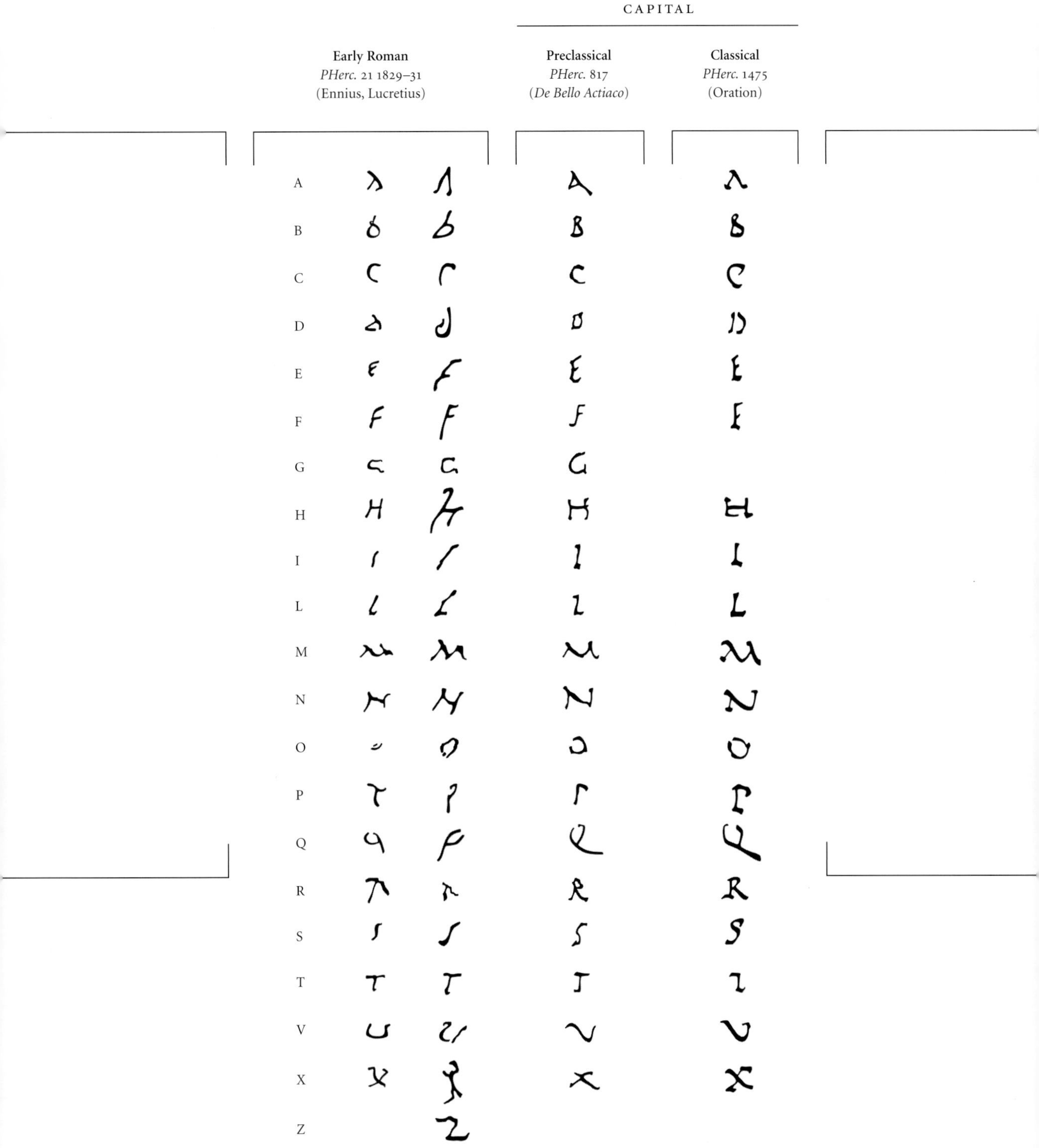
CAPITAL
Early Roman
PHerc. 21 1829–31
(Ennius, Lucretius)
Preclassical
PHerc. 817
(De Bello Actiaco)
Classical
PHerc. 1475
(Oration)
A
B
C
D
E
F
G
H
I
L
M
N
O
P
Q
R
S
T
V
X
Z

However unfair the initial disappointment after the rediscovery of the papyri that the Greek books were largely philosophy texts, the accompanying disappointment that there were not more Latin texts is entirely understandable. Still, the Latin papyri are far from uninteresting, although most of the sixty-two fragments, or rather, groupings of fragments, with *PHerc.* numbers are extremely exiguous. The description in the *Catalogo* for *PHerc.* 21 is typical: *non intero, poco leggibile, cattivo* ("incomplete, barely legible, in bad shape"). *PHerc.* 1066 is so *pessimo* that it is uncertain whether it is in fact Latin. Nonetheless, from such unpromising material, even from *PHerc.* 21, several interesting discoveries have been made.

PHerc. 817, *Carmen de Bello Actiaco* (The Battle of Actium)

This is the name given to the most interesting of the Latin texts, which attracted attention as soon as it was unrolled in 1805. It contains significant portions of fifty-six hexameter lines in eight columns, of which the last was given to Napoleon Bonaparte in 1809. The action of the poem takes place soon after the battle at Actium in 31 B.C. between Octavian (the future Emperor Augustus) and Antony and Cleopatra, who, sensing defeat, prepares for her suicide. The handwriting is one of the earliest examples of the Latin rustic capital style, which is a forerunner of italic (FIGS. 67, 68).[120] The scribe also added a number of punctuation and metrical signs, which fell out of favor in the medieval manuscripts.[121]

The desire to ascribe the poem to a known poet was not resisted, although there is very little on which to base a firm argument. The first candidate proposed for authorship and still a favorite of many is Gaius Rabirius, by whom we have very little, only five lines for sure, but since one brief fragment has Antony aware of his imminent death, Rabirius makes an obvious suspect. Some ancients, including Ovid, rated him highly but Quintilian, whose thumb-nail descriptions of poets hold up remarkably well, thought little of him. John Hayter favored Lucius Varius Rufus (see p. 43 and FIG. 67).[122] Cornelius Severus, the author of a verse *Roman History* (*Res romanae*) is another candidate; and Quintilian liked his poem on the war fought in Sicily earlier in the first century B.C. On the other hand, how good is the *Carmen de Bello Actiaco*? The author has mastered Vergilian metrics, but his imagery owes more to the later taste for the macabre. It may well be a second-rate poem by Rabirius or some other poetaster.

Here are columns five and six, in which Cleopatra VII, ruler of Egypt, has criminals put to death in various ways so that she may determine how she will end her own life:[123]

v . . . [dele]ctumqu[e loc]um quo·noxia turba co[i]ret·
praeberetque·suae·spectacula·tri[s]tia mortis· /
Qualis·ad ínstantís·aciés·cum tela·parantur·
signa·tubae·classesque·simul·terrestribus armís· /
est·facies·ea·visa·locí, cum saeva·coírent·   5
instrumenta·necis·v[a]rio·congesta·paratú /
und[i]que·sic·illúc campo·deforme·co[a]c[t]um
omne·vagabatur·leti genus· ómne·timoris· /

VI [Hic i]acet [absumptus f]erro·tu[m]et [il]le·ven[eno·] /
aut pendente [su]is·cervícibus·aspide·mollem·
labitur·in·somnum·trahiturque·libídine·mortis· /
percutit[·ad]flatu·brevis·hunc·sine·morsibus·anguis·
volnere·seu·t[e]nuí·pars·inlita·parva·venéni·   5
ocius·interem[i]t·laqueís·pars·cogitur·artís·
in[t]ersaeptam·animam·pressís·effundere·venis· /
i[m]mersisque·f[r]eto·clauserunt·guttura·fauces.

>—

[h]as·inter·strages·solio·déscendit·et·inter . . .
[. . .

Translation:

v   . . . and the place assigned, where the crowd of criminals would collect and provide sad spectacles of their
own deaths. Just as, for an army and fleet on the point of attack, weapons, flags, and trumpets are readied

FIGURE 69

Letteralogy: On the basis of the ink traces, the computer suggests the letters they may come from, which are indicated in this reconstruction by dotted lines. These letters were then identified as overlapping with a previously known fragment of Ennius *Annales* Book 6.183–85: ⌊Ne⌋c mi ⌊aurum posco nec mi pretium dederitis:⌋ | Non ⌊cauponantes bellum sed belligerantes⌋ | ferro, n⌊on auro vitam cernanum utrique⌋, "I ask not for gold for myself; you shall not pay me anything: Not haggling over war, but waging full battle, and with swords not gold—that's how we should fight for our lives." Letters enclosed in half brackets (⌊ ⌋) are those previously known. Reconstruction of *PHerc.* 21. From Knut Kleve, "Ennius in Herculaneum," *CErc* 20 (1990), fig. 3c. Reproduced by courtesy of Knut Kleve.

68

this is what the place looked like, as the cruel instruments of death were collected, brought together in varying stages of readiness. Thus, every kind of ugly death, every kind of ugly fear, was gathered there on the field.

VI   One man lies cut down by the sword; another is swollen with poison, or with an asp hanging on his throat he slips into sleep, led on by his lust for death; another a small basilisk strikes with his hisses alone, without a bite; or a tiny bit of poison smeared in a small wound does away with him more quickly; others are forced by tight nooses to pour forth their last breath through compressed passages; and others had their throats closed when they were immersed in water. In the midst of this slaughter she descended from her throne and in the midst of . . .

And we all know which of these deaths she chose for herself.

PHerc. 1829, 1830, 1831, Lucretius

Three papyri (only recently given numbers) were opened in the late 1980s. When Knut Kleve deciphered them and some isolated pieces from the same drawer, he discovered that they were fragments of four of the six books (1, 3, 4, and 5) of Lucretius's Epicurean poem *On the Nature of Things,* written in the early Roman script.[124] It is thus all but certain that there was a complete copy of all six books in the Villa. Since Lucretius is a poet, he fits in nicely with the other Latin literary texts found: Ennius, Caecilius, and the poem on Actium; but he obviously also belongs in any Epicurean library.[125] Lucretius remains an enigma, a mysterious figure whose life is largely unknown to us. It is probably an exaggeration to say, as Kleve does in the initial publication, that "the discovery links Lucretius firmly with the school in Herculaneum. Theories building on the assumption that Lucretius had no contact with contemporary Epicureanism suffer a serious set-back." The text is not the man, however; the latter may never have traveled south of Rome (his poem attests to some personal knowledge of the city) and the former could, for all we know, have been added to the library at any point between 40 B.C. (a reasonable guess for the date of Philodemos's death) and the eruption of A.D. 79.

The pieces are quite small and the writing as usual *illeggibile e cattivo* (illegible and bad). One is always greedy for more, but, still, it is an exciting discovery. How, though, was Kleve able to identify the exiguous scraps as the work of Lucretius? He does not explain how, other than to say that he made use of two standard concordances to Lucretius.[126] Kleve's fragment L, which belongs to the roll containing Book 1, reads as follows:

]O N D A M I [
] I . . [

Looking to that place in Book 1 where, approximately, the full text should be, one finds instead that the manuscript called o[blongus] has left a space of eight lines and that called Q[uadratus] indicates a lacuna with a cross. (These are the two chief medieval transcriptions of the now-lost original text.) These are standard ways scribes have of indicating that their master copy has been damaged. The letter *I* is frustratingly all that the papyrus gives us of this lost passage. A more meticulous scribe, like that of o, will give an indication of the length of the gap; others, like Q (and G, another good manuscript), will at least warn the reader that one or more lines are missing; and others, unfortunately, will not signal a lacuna at all. Since there are unmarked lacunae (as posited by editors; see immediately below) in o and Q, we must assume that the gap had been ignored by scribes prior to the scribe of their master copy. Fragment L gives us only the word [*qu*]*ondam,* but Kleve holds out the hope that with further work on the papyri, more may yet be read.

Another scrap from Herculaneum confirms an editorial alteration made by Hermann Diels in 1922. o and Q, the medieval manuscripts of Lucretius now in Leiden,[127] agree in giving two lines in Book 1 as follows (with the next line added):

praterea tellus quae corpora cumque alit auget	873
ex alienigenis, quae lignis exoriuntur	874
linquitur hic quaedam latitandi copia tenvis	875

Diels argued (i) that 873 and 874 should be transposed and (ii) that there is a lacuna immediately afterward; that is, the scribe carelessly omitted at least one line. On both counts, fragment H seems to prove that Diels was right. It reads as follows:

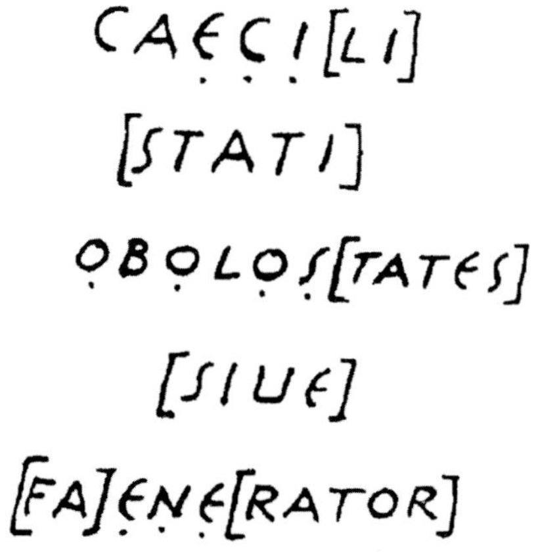

CAECI[LI]

[STATI]

OBOLOS[TATES]

[SIUE]

[FA]ENE[RATOR]

FIGURE 70
Reconstruction of the title of Caecilius's play *Obolostates, or Faenerator,* that is, *The Usurer,* in *PHerc. 78.* From *CErc 26* (1996), fig. 6, p. 12. Reproduced by courtesy of Knut Kleve.

$$]\,I\,G\,E\,N\,[$$
$$]\,L\,U\,S\cdot Q\,[$$
$$X\cdot U\,I\,R\,[$$

That is, 874 + 873 + letters that are not found in 875 but are rather traces of a previously unknown line (with the phrase, which Lucretius uses elsewhere, [e]x vir[ibus]). This is what all textual scholars live for, even if vindication comes, as in Diels's case, sixty-seven years after one's death.

PHerc. 21, Ennius

Several loose pieces from the same original roll overlap in a number of lines with previously known literary fragments from Book 6 of Ennius's *Annales;* it is safe to assume that two others that overlap with literary fragments, which are identified as having come only from the *Annales,* come from Book 6 as well.[128] When this papyrus was first opened in 1965, its badly damaged archaic letters made identification of the text impossible. In the next few years it was taken to be either a sacred text or a comedy. It was not until 1988 that Ennius was identified as the author (FIG. 69).

Ennius (239–169 B.C.) was widely admired in antiquity not only by ordinary readers but also by later poets, who paid him the highest homage (as it was understood in the ancient world) by openly adapting his lines. Ennius himself overtly took Homer over into rugged Latin hexameters, going so far as to claim that Homer visited him in a dream—*visus Homerus adesse poeta*—and told him that his, Homer's, soul now lived on in Ennius's body.[129] Thus, although many of his lines were worth quoting for their own poetic qualities or by later lexicographers or grammarians for their archaic features,[130] we owe the number of Ennius citations we have chiefly to ancient scholarly commentators eager to tell us where Ennius adapts Homer and where he in turn is adapted by others. Often, one English translation will adequately render Homer, Ennius, and Vergil. We thus have over 550 lines of Ennius's *Annales* alone, usually identified further by book number. Ennius modeled his *Annales* on prose annals that take the reader through historical events year by year. In this case, Ennius attempted nothing less than the complete history of Rome in fifteen books, down to the Aetolian War in 189 B.C., to which, some years later, he appended a further three books, updating his history to 171 B.C.

The present crop of fragments, in addition to locating two previously unplaced fragments in Book 6, also offers support for some readings over others.[131] These are not, admittedly, the most profound of revelations. The mere presence of Ennius in the library is surprise enough. Could the Villa have had only one of the eighteen books, the one detailing the war in the 270s with Pyrrhus, him of the Pyrrhic victories? Possibly, but not likely. Any hope that the Latin library of the Villa will be discovered should include the expectation that one or more complete book rolls will yield at least one complete book of the *Annales*.

PHerc. 78, Caecilius Statius

Although a complete roll, *PHerc. 78* was long regarded as hopeless—*illeggibile, pessimo,* says the *Catalogo*—yet it finally began to give up its secrets to the new techniques (pp. 58f.). Its end-title identifies author and work:[132]

C A E C I [L I]

[S T A T I]

O B O L O S [T A T E S]

[S I V E]

[F A] E N E [R A T O R][133]

"The *Obolostates* or *Faenerator* of Caecilius Statius," the alternate titles being, respectively, the Greek and Latin words for *usurer* (FIG. 70). Caecilius was a well-known adaptor of Greek comedy for Roman audiences. Many of his plays retain their original Greek titles; only this one has both the Greek original and its Latin translation. The two famous authors of Latin comedy are Plautus and Terence, but fragments of others, including Caecilius, have long been known.[134] It is fortunate that the title can be read, for none of the previously known fragments has been found with a title, although further work remains to be done.

On the basis of what he has so far read, Kleve sums up the likely plot: "I think the play is about a young man who has fallen in love with a girl. The girl, however, is in the clutches of a pimp. To ransom his sweetheart the lover borrows money from a usurer, but is unable to pay back the loan which is rapidly growing because of high interest. He asks his father for help, but in vain. The father timidly refuses to spend money against the will of the other heir, the lover's brother. The bad brother seems unaware that he is only entitled to one half of the family fortune." In other words, a typical domestic plot of the sort first developed in what is now called New Comedy, the fullest Greek examples of which are by Menander.[135]

Caecilius's play also contains a trial and, as often in Greek and then Roman comedy, a faithful and clever slave. While Kleve will eventually publish more, it seems that this roll contains only 400–500 lines of verse, that is, only half of the comedy.

These four poems are the most exciting Latin discoveries to date. One other roll contains scraps of hexameter (*PHerc.* 399), but is too small to be identified further. A second roll containing hexameters (*PHerc.* 397) has been lost, although eighteenth-century copies exist in Naples and in the Bodleian Library.[136] There are also scraps of Latin prose. For example:

PHerc. 371 "is remarkably regular and careful, like the the letters of an inscription" (Lindsay), which suggests a literary text of some worth, although, if so, it is one no longer extant. Nor do we have enough to discern even its general subject matter.

PHerc. 394 has been interpreted as a panegyric on Augustus, since it directly addresses someone (the second-person singular possessive adjective *tui* occurs) and contains a tightly packed cluster of geographic names, such as Germania, Ethiopia, and Macedonia, all of political interest to Augustus, as well as a reference to the tetrarch of the Jews (*Iudaeos tetra*[*rch . .*])

PHerc. 413 seems to have a speaker's name twice in the margin, once before line 2 and again before line 7, abbreviated to *Cum*, possibly standing for Cumanus (= someone from Cumae) or the proper name Cumelius. This seems, therefore, to be part of a prose dialogue.

In sum, as we learn from Kleve, "30 of the Latin papyri are written in Early Roman script and so probably belong to the first century B.C. 11 papyri are written in preclassical capital script and so probably belong to the last part of the first century B.C. (from 31 B.C.). 17 papyri are written in classical capital script and so probably belong to the first century A.D. (until 79 A.D.). The distribution of the scripts indicates that the library in the Papyrus Villa has been an active library, kept up to date to the bitter end."[137]

FIGURE 71

Plato and his students, in a Pompeian mosaic of the early first century B.C. Plato sits under a tree reading from a book roll and pointing to a celestial globe. Aristotle is at the right, the only figure to turn his back on Plato, although he cannot resist looking back at him. The setting is probably meant to be Plato's Academy, outside the walls of Athens, which can be seen in the background. Naples, Museo Archeologico Nazionale, inv. 124545. See Karl Schefold, *Bildnisse der antiken Dichter, Redner und Denker* (Basel, 1997) 294–96.

The Greek Texts

The Greek library comprises Hellenistic philosophical treatises, and nothing but. Most are Epicurean, although there are also some Stoic texts, present almost certainly to provide handy sources of philosophical errors for an Epicurean author. For many of the rolls, authorship is fixed by end-titles or overlaps with otherwise known texts; for others, authorship can be reasonably guessed. The presence of duplicate copies of many works suggests that this was a philosopher's working library;[138] and since the library was formed in the lifetime of Philodemos, whose works are represented most fully, the philosophy texts almost certainly were part of his personal library.[139]

A working library is built up over a working lifetime. Since Philodemos was born in the small but cultured Greek city of Gadara (now Um Qeis, in Jordan), his formal introduction to philosophy most likely began in Athens, the home of all the major philosophical schools from the fourth century B.C. to the sixth century A.D.: Platonism in the Academy, Aristotelianism in the Lyceum (Lykeion), Stoicism in the Porch (Stoa), and Epicureanism in the Garden (Kēpos; FIG. 71). For the last, the cloistered idea of a garden where one could withdraw from the cares of the outside world became a governing metaphor; everywhere Epicureans regularly met for philosophical conviviality became their "Garden."

If Philodemos attended lectures given by teachers of the other schools in Athens, he wiped it from the record. In the texts we have, he is a committed Epicurean. When he left Athens, he took with him some basic texts of Epikouros and some of his followers. According to Guglielmo Cavallo, who has made the most detailed study of the handwriting and other pertinent physical details of the book rolls (all part of the craft of palaeography), the oldest texts in the Villa's library belong to Epikouros's *On Nature* (*Peri physeos*), and some may have been transcribed during Epikouros's own lifetime (341–270 B.C.; FIG. 72).[140] Books 2 and 28 are expressly identified; others say merely "Epikouros *On Nature*"; while still others may safely be assigned to this work even though the end-title is missing. In all, Cavallo assigns seven rolls to the

FIGURE 72

PHerc. 1413, cornice 2, Multispectral image of a fragment from an unknown book of Epikouros *On Nature*, which is concerned with the meaning of time. This papyrus was written by a professional scribe in the late second or early first century B.C. See Raffaele Cantarella and Graziano Arrighetti, "Il libro *Sul Tempo* (*PHerc.* 1413) dell' opera di Epicuro *Sulla Natura*," *CErc* 2 (1972): 5–46. ©2002 Biblioteca Nazionale 'Vittorio Emanule III' di Napoli and the Center for the Preservation of Ancient Religious Texts (CPART) at Brigham Young University, Provo, UT, USA. All rights reserved. Reproduced by permission of the Ministero per i Beni e le Attività Culturali.

earliest group, his Group A. Of these, four were written by the same scribe (Anonymous I; FIG. 73). Altogether, Cavallo has identified seventeen Groups (A–R [there is no J]), and thirty-four different distinct scribal hands. One of these, Anonymous XXII, may have signed his name: Poseidonax the son of Biton, but other suggestions have been made to explain the placing of a proper name at the end of *PHerc.* 1426, a roll containing Philodemos's *Rhetoric*. A particularly valuable result of Cavallo's research has been to correct earlier attempts to assign to Philodemos treatises that Cavallo can now date to the second century B.C., such as *PHerc.* 176 (see p. 81). Cavallo has also put to rest the lingering romantic notion that among the papyri we had *la mano di Filodemo*, a book written in Philodemos's own hand. All, it seems, were written by professional scribes.

Other rolls, written later, add to what may be Epikouros's *On Nature*, so that we now have identified portions of Books 2, 11, 14, 15, 25, 28, and 34. In addition, Philodemos quotes from books 3, 12, and 24, so that we now have, directly or indirectly, excerpts from ten of the thirty-seven books, the original total, as we learn from Diogenes Laertios. Other rolls clearly belonging to *On Nature* will, when they are opened and read, fill in some of the gaps.[141] The rolls of *On Nature* can themselves be further supplemented by some passages where Philodemos, in yet other Herculaneum rolls, cites from this work by name and, often, book number; for example, in his *On Piety* he says that "in Book 12 of *On Nature* he [Epikouros] says that the first people [in human history] arrived at conceptions of imperishable external entities" (i.e., gods; Book 1, col. 8.225–31 in the edition of Dirk Obbink, whose translations I use). This is an example of a literary fragment (of Epikouros) embedded within a papyrus fragment (of Philodemos; see n. 128).

The importance of the Herculaneum papyri for our knowledge of what is likely to have been Epikouros's most important work is underlined by the fact that previously we had very few citations, and these were mostly brief summaries that omitted his philosophical argumentation; for example, Plutarch's anti-Epicurean *Against Colotes* 1114a, which tells us what we already knew from other sources, that at the very beginning of *On Nature* Epikouros said that "the nature of things consists [only] of bodies and void," which Lucretius versified as *omnis ut est igitur per se natura duabus | constitit in rebus: nam corpora sunt et inane* (*On the Nature of Things* 1.419–20).[142]

It has not been easy to discern the overall arrangement of so large a work now in tatters, but David Sedley argues that one of the three extant letters of Epikouros, his *Letter to Herodotos*, summarizes the contents of *On Nature*, books 1–13:

My guess is that the Περὶ Φύσεως [*On Nature*] started out by expounding what Epicurus, to judge from the *Letter to Herodotus,* regarded as his chief doctrines on physics and cosmology (Books I–XIII), then set out systematically to refute rival physical theories (XIVff.), later moved on to canonic (a group of books round XXVIII?), and later still to psychological, and hence presumably ethical, consequences of Epicurean physics (XXXIIff.?). Epikouros's view of it as an ordered work would be consistent with some such broad division into physics, canonic, and ethics.[143]

In addition to this central work of Epikouros, the Villa's library has given us works by some of Epikouros's disciples: Metrodoros *On Wealth* (*PHerc.* 200); Polystratos *On Irrational Contempt of Popular Opinion* and *On Philosophy,* Book 1; Kolotes *Against Plato's "Lysis"* and *Against Plato's "Euthydemos";* and Karneiskos *Philistas,* Book 2. Closer to Philodemos's time is Demetrios Lakon (i.e., "the Laconian"), who was a contemporary of Philodemos's teacher in Athens, Zenon of Sidon— a Phoenician city; he is to be distinguished from Zenon of Kition (in Cyprus), the founder of Stoicism—three of whose rolls fall into Cavallo's Group B, which, since these display signs of having been written in the second century B.C., again suggests that Philodemos carried these with him when he left Athens. One is labeled "Demetrios *On Poetry,* Book 2," which strongly suggests that the library also contained Book 1 of the same work. Another roll has only the last few letters of the title, but [*On Geome*]*try* is a reasonable guess. Other works by Demetrios fall into other of Cavallo's groups, including *On the Problems of Polyainos,* and *On Some Views of Epikouros.* A previously unknown work of Zenon was recently discovered; in it, Zenon replies to an earlier criticism of his *On Geometrical Proofs.*[144]

There are also two works by someone other than an Epicurean, the Stoic Khrysippos's *On Foreknowledge,* Book 1, and *Logical Investigations.* Philodemos, however, refers to so many (at least sixteen) of Khrysippos's works by name in the papyri already opened, that it is easy to believe that other works by Khrysippos will be found.[145] It has to be admitted, though, that even if Philodemos did in fact have on hand every philosophical work he cites by name, his personal library could have been diminished over the long period between his death ca. 40 B.C. and the eruption. Since no Greek could do otherwise, certainly not one who wrote on literary theory, he also quotes and refers to poets, from Homer to the obscure fourth-century poet Telestes. Strangely, even though Philodemos's own poems clearly continue in the tradition of Greek epigram written from the third to the first century B.C., he nowhere alludes to any

FIGURE 73

PHerc. 1479/1417, cornice 11. The tops (on 1497) and bottoms (on 1417) of columns 6–10 of Epikouros *On Nature* Book 28 (multispectral image). Each column is ca. 4.5 cm (1¾ in.) wide. Owing to the breaking of the roll into two, lines are lost in the middle of each column, but the text runs continuously from the bottom of one column to the top of the next, and in some columns the loss is minimal. This papyrus was copied by a professional scribe during the lifetime of Epikouros. For a translation, see David Sedley, "Epikouros *On Nature* Book XXVIII," *CErc* 3 (1973): 49–54. © 2002 Biblioteca Nazionale 'Vittorio Emanule III' di Napoli and the Center for the Preservation of Ancient Religious Texts (CPART) at Brigham Young University, Provo, UT, USA. All rights reserved. Reproduced by permission of the Ministero per i Beni e le Attività Culturali.

76

Hellenistic poet, many of whom—most notably Kallimakhos—wrote highly self-referential and sophisticated poetry that alluded to the literary theories that Philodemos discusses in his prose works.

PHILODEMOS AND HIS TEXTS

Philodemos is explicitly identified as the author of forty-four rolls, and he has been conjectured to be the author of 120 more—or, rather, sections of rolls, since many of these 120 will surely prove to belong to others, so that the total number of actual book rolls is less than this. Still, the bulk of the library so far identified proves to be by one philosopher. Here, then, is perhaps the best reason for believing that the Villa's library belonged to Philodemos in his lifetime. Whatever one may think of him, he never figured large in anybody's account of Greek philosophy in general nor in Epicureanism in particular.[146] Who other than Philodemos himself would collect multiple copies of some of his works? Furthermore, many of the texts in the library seem more like notes taken down at Zenon's lectures and less like published treatises.

Here then is an abbreviated overview of the prose works, either explicitly or very likely, by Philodemos.[147] In some cases, titles are no more than likely conjectures; in others, Philodemos's authorship is assumed but not actually specified. It will be convenient to arrange his works by subject matter.

On the History of Philosophy

Diogenes Laertios attests to a work by Philodemos with the title *Syntaxis tōn Philosophōn*, which roughly translates as *Systematic Arrangement* (or *Index*) *of Philosophers*.[148] Interestingly, Diogenes tells us in Book 10 of his history of Greek philosophers, which is devoted to Epikouros, that Philodemos wrote about Epikouros in Book 10 of *his* history of philosophy. This may be no more than coincidence, but it allows for the possibility that Diogenes modeled his *Lives and Opinions of Eminent Philosophers* on Philodemos's earlier account.[149] The title *Syntaxis tōn Philosophōn* has not been found in Herculaneum, but some of the scrolls have reasonably been taken to be individual books of this comprehensive work, even though no author/title has been found, with the partial exception of *su*[on the broken end-title of *PHerc.* 1018, which could well be the beginning of *Sy*[*ntaxis*.

PHerc. 1021 and 164 are two copies written down at different dates of a book dealing with the Academy from Plato to Antiochos of Askalon—whose lectures Cicero attended—and his brother Aristos, who succeeded him as head (scholarch) of the Academy in 68 or 67 B.C.[150] Indeed, it is only thanks to this work of Philodemos that it could finally be established that Antiochos did in fact become scholarch of the Academy rather than, as had been thought, the founder of a rival academy. Aristos was successful in Rome, obtaining Marcus Brutus as his patron, but he was thought little of as a philosopher. Plutarch refers to him as "a man for his learning inferior indeed to many of the philosophers, but for the evenness of his temper and steadiness of his conduct equal to the best" (*Life of Brutus* 2.2, trans. John Dryden, whose rendering of Plutarch's *Lives* has never been bettered).

Both *PHerc.* 1021 (in fifty-nine columns) and 164 (in thirty-three) are fragmentary, as usual, but the various pieces supplement each other and occasionally overlap. They are not, however, simply two copies of the same text: *PHerc.* 1021 was written earlier, about 70 B.C., and frequently sends the reader (or scribe) to revisions written on the other side of the papyrus. *PHerc.* 164 was written later, perhaps after Philodemos's death, but taking the revisions into account.

In general, Philodemos balances praise of Plato with blame, as befits a lover of literature who is also an Epicurean.[151] Note, for example, his summary of Plato's activity as a writer of philosophical dialogues: "[Plato] himself introduced many things, thanks to which—if I may speak freely of the results of this—he, more than any man, both added to philosophy and undid it. For by writing dialogues, he encouraged an almost uncountable number to take it up, but some of them he also made philosophize superficially, diverting them down an obvious path" (col. 1.5–18).

History of the Stoics

Platonism and Aristotelianism were largely for those prepared to devote their lives to the study of philosophy; or in some cases for those who delighted in abstruse argument for its own sake. It was Epicureanism and Stoicism, the two main Hellenistic schools of philosophy, that competed for wide audiences by presenting much, though certainly not all, of their teachings (oral and written) on a more popular level than did the Academy and the Lyceum. It is scarcely surprising, then, that Philodemos, following his teacher Zenon, directed many arguments against one or another Stoic.

PHerc. 1018, like the account of the Academy, speaks more of philosophers than of their beliefs and is likewise ordered chronologically. It too, therefore, seems to be part of the *Syntaxis of Philosophers.*[152] The tone is rather neutral, too, like that on the Academy and very much unlike that found in Philodemos's other works on the Stoics, where their views come in for sharp criticism. In this work, however, Philodemos feels comfortable calling Apollonios of Ptolemaïs, a contemporary of Philodemos, "my friend" (col. 78.3). The first legible column of *PHerc.* 1018's seventy-nine columns opens in the middle of a discussion of Zenon of Kition's theory on the nature of the soul. Since Zenon was the founder of Stoicism, not too much has been lost from the beginning of this book of the *Syntaxis.* Still, as other biographies in this work show, Philodemos would have begun with Zenon's biography, which would have included his physical description and when and where he was born (Kition on Cyprus in a year when Ktesikles was archon in Athens; i.e., 334/3 B.C.). We do learn that he enjoyed figs (FIG. 74) and sunbathing (*heliasmos,* a word that appears only here in all of known Greek literature and too newly discovered to have been entered in any Greek dictionary), probably to make up for all the hours he spent in the library (see Diogenes Laertios's *Life of Zenon,* where we learn that an oracle told him "to take on the complexion of the dead, which he immediately knew meant reading ancient authors," 7.2. Scholars, take note.).

After Zenon, Philodemos treats nine more Stoics, including Kleanthes and Khrysippos, finishing with a relatively extensive account of Panaitios of Rhodes, up until his death in 109 B.C. The roll ends with a list of Panaitios's students, at least two of whom Philodemos knew personally: Apollonios of Ptolemaïs and Thibron (col. 76.6). Philodemos would have known Zenon's views directly from his writings, but the biographical details, as he tells us himself, came from another contemporary student of Panaitios: Stratokles of Rhodes. Again, one wonders whether Philodemos spent time in Rhodes (see n. 139).

Although more polemical in tone than historical, two works that contain matters of historical interest may be considered here. *PHerc.* 155, identified as "Philodemos *On the Stoics,*" overlaps with *PHerc.* 339, so that the latter's incomplete title, "Philodemos *On the* [. . .]," can readily be filled in.[153] In this work, Philodemos attacks Zenon of Kition for his *Republic.* This title—*Politeia* in Greek—could also be translated as *Constitution,* but this would hide the fact that Zenon was engaged in a dialogue

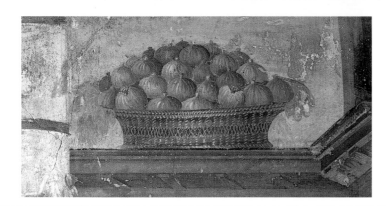

with Plato's work of the same name.[154] Thus, even the minor matter of women's dress, including the question whether women, like men, should strip for athletics, was discussed by Zenon, just as it was by Plato (and as it was also by Zenon's teacher, Krates the Cynic), for which he was criticized by Philodemos. Other unnamed Stoic contemporaries came in for criticism, as is usual in Philodemos's polemical philosophical accounts.

Another work with an incomplete title is *PHerc*. 1005: "Philodemos *Against the* [...]." Some have filled in the blank with *Stoics*, but others have gone with *Sophists*, which would refer not to the famous Sophists of fifth-century Greece but to Epicureans who, in the view of other Epicureans, such as Philodemos, have deviated from true thinking. Since, however, the preposition here translated as "against" could just as well be translated as "to," in the sense that one addresses a letter "to" a friend, the most recent edition of this text is called *Agli amici di scuola*, "*To* the friends of the School."[155] The work is obviously too fragmentary for us to get an overview, but it is clear that Philodemos directs much of his polemics to fellow Epicureans: "I do indeed agree, as I said in the beginning, that some of those self-styled Epicureans say and write many things that they have patched together, but also much that is their own, although not in accord with the [true Epicurean] writings."

History of Epicureanism

This subject, not surprisingly, was treated in a number of works. Two books of *On Epikouros* are partially extant (*PHerc*. 1232 and 1289, each explicitly labeled "Philodemos *On Epikouros*," the latter also as "Book 2").[156] Another roll (*PHerc*. 176) whose title is lost likewise details the early history of Epicureanism and quotes from some of Epikouros's letters. Since it was, according to Guglielmo Cavallo, written in the second century B.C., it cannot be by Philodemos, who did, however, write a similar work, with the unusually long title *Treatise Concerning the Records of Epikouros and Some Others* (*PHerc*. 1418 and 310), usually called simply by the first word of its Greek title, *Pragmateiai*. This too contains fragments of otherwise lost letters of Epikouros.[157]

Some of these letters were never intended for publication, although Philodemos quoted from one of them to illustrate with what evenness of temper Epikouros faced his death: "Today is the seventh day I have been unable to urinate and I have pains that signal death" (*Pragmateiai*, *PHerc*. 1418, col.

FIGURE 74
Basket with purple and green figs. Wall-painting from the dining room (*triclinium*) of the Villa of Poppaea in Oplontis.
Photo: Foglia, Naples.

31.5–10). Epikouros was a voluminous writer, and he was happy to write at length to his friends about his philosophical views. Three of these letters were fortunately copied in their entirety by Diogenes Laertios in his long biography of Epikouros: *To Pythokles,* on cosmology and meteorology; *To Herodotos,* on physics, and *To Menoikeus,* on ethics. These remain the only complete extant works of Epikouros. Fragments of other letters have come down to us embedded in the texts of Seneca, Plutarch, Stobaios, and others. Because Philodemos, as an Epicurean himself, found reason to quote from them, the Herculaneum papyri have given us additional fragments.

Since Philodemos's audience for these treatises would be, for the most part, his fellow Epicureans, he would as a matter of course have nothing but praise for their master, with the explicit corollary that they should continue to emulate him and continue to adhere to his doctrines. This praise of, and call to emulate, Epikouros is familiar to readers of Lucretius; see, for example, the opening words of Book 3: "O you who were the first to have the power to raise high so clear a torch in the deepest darkness, shedding light on the blessings of light—I follow you, o glory of the Greek people, . . . I am eager to emulate you."

Philodemos frequently finds reason to criticize the Epicureans living on Rhodes for having deviated from the master's teachings. *On Epikouros* also contains a passage in which we learn of Epikouros's "feasts," held on the twentieth of every month, which were intended to bring together in philosophical friendship not only those already adhering to his views but also sympathetic "outsiders":

> [But Epikouros says] that he invites these very people to join in a feast, just as he invites others—all those who are members of his household and he asks them to exclude none of the outsiders who are well disposed both to him and to his friends. In doing this [he says], they will not be engaged in gathering the masses, something which is a form of meaningless demagoguery and unworthy of the natural philosopher; rather, in practicing what is congenial to their nature, they will remember all those who are well disposed to us so that they can join on their blessed day[?] in making the sacred offerings that are fitting to . . .

This passage sheds much light on some other puzzling descriptions of the "Feast of the Twentieth," when, as it is not too strong to call it, the cult of Epikouros was celebrated, both while he was alive and well into Philodemos's day.[158]

Epikouros was born on the twentieth day of the month of Gamelion (roughly equal to January).

The practices described in this and the parallel texts present us with some apparent paradoxes or at any rate inconsistencies with what Epikouros was thought to teach elsewhere. In one of his epigrams, Philodemos invites Piso, one of the sympathetic outsiders, to join in the Epicurean good cheer:

> Tomorrow, friend Piso, your musical comrade drags you to his modest
>> digs at three in the afternoon,
> feeding you at your annual visit to the Twentieth. If you will miss udders
>> and Bromian wine *mis en bouteilles* in Chios,
> yet you will see faithful comrades, yet you will hear things far sweeter
>> than the land of the Phaeacians.[159]
> And if you ever turn your eye our way too, Piso, instead of a modest
>> Twentieth we shall lead a richer one.

Since Philodemos invites Piso to his home and furthermore calls it a modest one (an Epicurean *topos*; Vergil does the same thing in his early poem to the Epicurean Siron), he clearly was not living in the Villa dei Papiri at the time (if ever). The poem is also clearly not only an invitation to the Twentieth but also an oblique request for patronage. Philodemos cleverly uses the Homeric word for "comrade" (*hetaros*) as a synonym for *philos*, "friend," which had an almost technical status with the Garden for the relationship between fellow Epicureans; *philos* also equates with the Latin *amicus*, which in turn was the technical term for the patron-client relationship that Philodemos seeks from Piso. Thus Philodemos deftly asks Piso to be a "friend" in the ordinary, the Epicurean, and the Roman senses of the word. *Hetaros* is also the word used by Odysseus of *his* comrades.

On the subject of Epikouros's establishment of the Twentieth, however, ancients, and some moderns, were quick to find fault. How could he encourage a cult of himself when he elsewhere described the gods of the Greek pantheon as mortal and as material as any earthly substance? How could he encourage feasts when elsewhere he urged simplicity in food as well as in other matters?[160] How could he urge his followers to honor him on his birthdate when elsewhere he famously said "Live quietly"? Surely, as Plutarch and others said, he was a hypocrite. As we shall see, his views on poetry were likewise subject to misinterpretation.

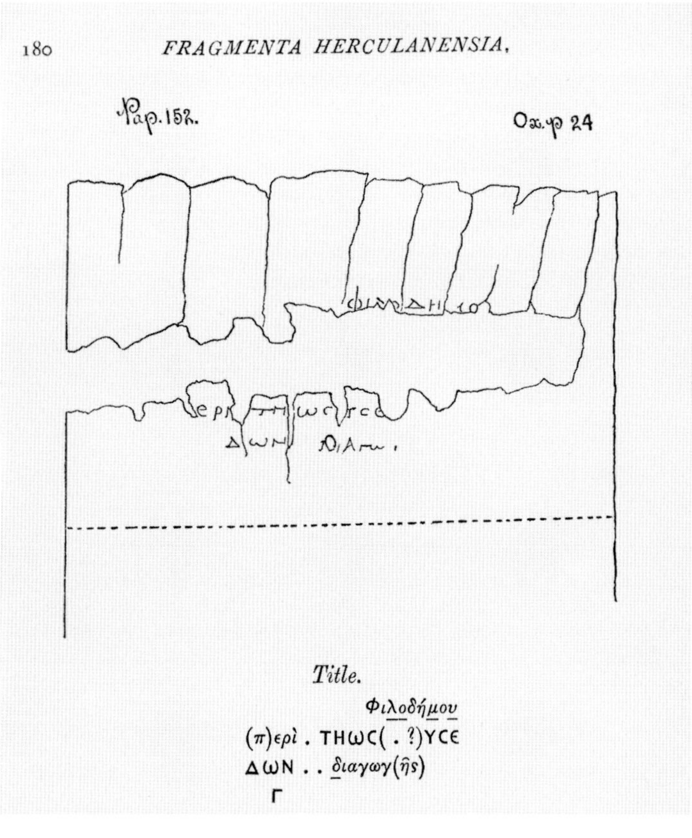

FIGURE 75

Disegno of the title of *PHerc.* 152/157. Philodemos's name
is clear; given the nature of the work itself, the title can be
restored to read *On the Gods*. A mark below this has been
read as Γ (gamma) and interpreted either as "Book 3" (since
gamma is the third letter of the alphabet) or as part of a stichometric or columnar numeration; others read the figure as
Z (zeta), with reference to Philodemos's teacher Zenon. From
Walter Scott, *Fragmenta Herculanensia* (Oxford, 1885) 180.

On Theology

In his historical writings, Philodemos keeps very much to a chronological arrangement. In his more argumentative mode, his practice is to outline the views of others, that is, non-Epicureans, and only then to offer counterarguments. This may not strike us as the most efficient way of doing things—Plato and Aristotle, for example, dispute arguments almost immediately—but this wide separation between the initial statement of a philosopher's views and the counterargument can be quite useful to the papyrologist editor since this modus operandi calls for more repetition than would be the case if Philodemos replied immediately. Many gaps in the papyri have thus been successfully filled by drawing from such repetitions spaced over wide distances.

Three (or possibly only two) works fall clearly into the category of theological treatises: *On the Gods' Way of Life, On the Gods,* and *On Piety.* The problem of how many texts there are is due to gaps in *PHerc.* 152/157 (one roll, now in two separately numbered pieces), whose fragmentary title reads "Philodemos, *On the . . . Gods' Way of Life.*" A trace of a letter after this title has been read by some as the Greek letter gamma, i.e., [Book] 3, but others have read this as a zeta, which could be the first letter of Zenon, who is often identified in Philodemos's titles as the source for the treatise in question. If so, this would be the third work on this subject. Still others, who have identified the letter as a gamma, have taken it to be a stichometric sign (see p. 48). For all the disagreement, however, this work has regularly been considered the third book of Philodemos's *On the Gods,* but on the basis of the evidence we have, that must remain at best only a reasonable inference (FIG. 75).[161]

The Epicureans believe that the gods live their lives quite apart from, and unconcerned with, ours. There is, then, no need for us to fear them, for if they interfered with our lives, they would be disturbing their own perfect happiness. Philodemos's treatise *On the Gods,* Book 1, has

*Pap.*152.   Ox.φ 24

ιερ[...]ωσ[ι]σα
Δ[ω]ν[ ] Δ[Αℸω]

Title.

Φιλοδήμου
(π)ερὶ . ΤΗωϹ(. ?)ΥϹΕ
ΔωΝ . . διαγωγ(ῆς)
Γ

some technical bones to pick with specific philosophers representing different schools of thought: Dionysios the Stoic, Ekhekles the Cynic, and Eudoxos the Hedonist (who was also criticized by Aristotle in his *Nicomachean Ethics*).[162] Philodemos calls them *philoi aphiletoi*, "friends who are no friends," which, in addition to being as unfriendly as it sounds, is especially pointed in a text like this, concerned to show that the gods exist in a perfect state of friendship with each other, one that provides mortals with a divine paradigm. Our goal, then, both individually and among like-minded friends, is "likeness to god," almost a technical term in Epicurean philosophy.

Another book concerning the gods concentrates on the proper attitude to maintain toward them, which naturally leads to further discussion of their nature: *On Piety* was originally on two rolls, but it is now broken into many parts with many different inventory numbers—Roll 1: *PHerc.* 1787//1098,[163] 229, 437/242, and 1610; and Roll 2: *PHerc.* 242, 247, 433, 1088, 1428, 1609, 1610, and 1648—and in two sets of *disegni* in Oxford and Naples. The interconnectedness of these many pieces is established by their having been written by the same hand (when the original still exists), by an occasional physical join, and by the common subject matter. As FIGURE 76 shows, I have simplified the numeration, in that some *PHerc.* numbers themselves divide into fragment numbers that were assigned before their relative order was established.

Epikouros's theory of the gods was based on his atomic theory: like everything else in the universe (except the vacuum) the gods were matter; that is, made up of atoms. Still, gods were gods and had to be distinguished in sometimes tortuous ways from all other matter. Before the discovery of the Herculaneum papyri, our knowledge of Epikouros's theology derived in large part from his enemies, who found it easy to charge him with varying degrees of hypocrisy, inconsistency, and outright lying. It was in fact largely to defend Epikouros from such charges that Philodemos wrote these works. Because of the gaps in the texts, not all answers are forthcoming, but they have greatly advanced our knowledge of the Epicurean gods. (The gods speak Greek, by the way, since, as nobody can deny, this is the language best designed to express the philosophical thoughts happily indulged in by all divine beings for all eternity.)

Thus, *On Piety* begins with Epikouros's arguments for the existence of gods, something most philosophers, let alone ordinary folk, are content to take for granted. It continues with examples of Epikouros's participation in public acts of religious piety, which is as much a defense of Epikouros as

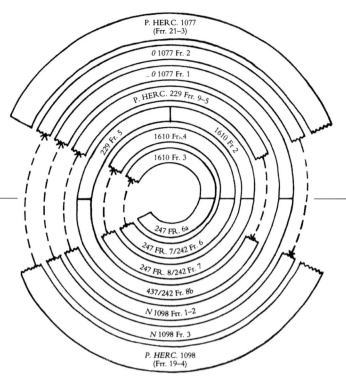

P. HERC. 1077
(Frr. 21–3)

0 1077 Fr. 2

0 1077 Fr. 1

P. HERC. 229 Frr. 9–5

229 Fr. 5

1610 Fr. 4

1610 Fr. 2

1610 Fr. 3

247 FR. 6a

247 FR. 7/242 Fr. 6

247 FR. 8/242 Fr. 7

437/242 Fr. 8b

N 1098 Frr. 1–2

N 1098 Fr. 3

P. HERC. 1098
(Frr. 19–4)

it is a working definition of piety. Similarly, although there were in fact very few declared atheists among Greek philosophical writers (atheism was a rather dangerous thing to avow), *On Piety,* Part 1, takes issue with several atheist positions and criticizes some for doing what others had accused Epikouros of, concealing their atheism.[164]

In Part 2 of *On Piety,* Philodemos deals with the ways in which poets have described the gods, none of which was in accord with the way Epikouros thought of them. After all, his picture of a quiet and peaceful conclave of deities who want nothing to do with the messy company of mortals is hardly the stuff of classical Greek poetry, which delights in describing gods who like nothing better than to respond to slights from mortals, some of them engaging in physical combat and sexual intercourse with each other and with mortals. For Epikouros, however, even a straightforward address in the form of a prayer is ineffectual, since the gods are not to be disturbed by our petty affairs.

This part of *On Piety* was closely paraphrased by Cicero in his work *On the Nature of Gods,* which helps us to follow Philodemos's overall argument. The two texts are so close that Hermann Diels, in his collection of writings on early Greek (largely pre-Socratic) thought, was able to print the two texts in parallel columns (FIG. 77).

On Logic

One fragmentary work touches on knowledge and its relation to perception and intellect: *PHerc.* 1389, "Philodemos *Concerning Proof.* From Zenon's lectures. Book 3 [and a now-missing line count]." As usual, the Epicurean view is defended against those of its opponents, in this case the Peripatetics (that is, the school of Aristotle), Stoics, and "some of the Epicureans here," although we do not know where "here" is. It need not indicate the place where the work was written, since it can just as easily be refer-

FIGURE 76
Layout of a reconstructed papyrus roll containing Philodemos's *On Piety.* Note how the fragments were numbered from the inside out as the *scorze* of the various pieces were separated (after transcription), a process that led to the text being read in reverse order (see pp. 52f.). From Dirk Obbink, *Philodemos* On Piety, *Part 1* (Oxford, 1996), fig. 2, p. 43. By permission of Oxford University Press.

ring to a place previously mentioned in the text. The word *apodeixis,* here translated "proof" and used by mathematicians in the strict sense, is distinguished by Epikouros from *epilogismos,* which is a less logical though still valid form of argumentation best translated as "empirical inference."

Another roll, *PHerc.* 1003, may be a second copy of this work, since its end-title reads "Philodemos *On the* [*Lectures*] *of Zenon,* Book 3," and it too is concerned with matters of proof.

The most complete book of this nature, however, is *PHerc.* 1065, "Philodemos *On Ph*[*ai*]*n*[*omen*]*a and Signs,*" although it becomes clear from the work itself that a more accurate rendering would be *On Phainomena, that is, Signs from Which One Can Infer, and How.* In fact, the best edition renders the title as *On Methods of Inference.*[165] Although there are some detached fragments, thirty-eight columns of almost continuous text exist, with relatively few lacunae, some of which can be filled in from the eighteenth-century copies where the papyrus has suffered damage since then.

As usual, the work polemically defends Epikouros's positions from attacks by Stoics. Philodemos, however, as in the shorter works on logic, is content to lay out the arguments of other Epicureans, in this case, not only Zenon's, but also those of Bromios and of Demetrios Lakon (see p. 75). Perhaps Philodemos felt that he himself had little to contribute to the difficult subject of logical inference. The basic question is how to argue from what we perceive (phenomena) to what we do not. It is not enough to say as the pre-Socratic philosopher Anaxagoras once pithily stated: "Phenomena: Sight of the Unseen." The particular features of any one class may mislead us as to what is true of the class in general, especially if we want to know about individuals of this class we have never seen, because, for example, they are or may be in Africa or India. Just because there are figs in Italy and Greece, we should not infer that they exist everywhere (col. 18). It does, on the other hand, seem reasonable to infer that since every man we see is mortal, then men everywhere are mortal (col. 23).

Unusual or unique objects may throw logical monkey wrenches into empirical arguments; "for example, the man in Alexandria half a cubit high [ca. 11 in.], with a colossal head that could be beaten with a hammer, who used to be exhibited by the embalmers; . . .and the person in Crete who was 48 cubits tall [ca. 88 ft.!], by inference from the bones that were found" (col. 4, trans. De Lacy and De Lacy).[166] Philodemos, who very likely saw the half-cubit high man when he was in Alexandria also seems to have made him the subject of one of his epigrams, although all that is left of this poem are the first three words: "O hammers, head . . ."

FIGURE 77

In his work *On the Nature of the Gods,* Cicero so closely
follows Philodemos's text of *On Piety* that a modern editor
found it convenient to align similar passages in parallel
columns. Shown here is a passage where both authors speak
of the Stoics' attempts to assimilate the stories found in poets
to their own doctrines. From Hermann Diels, *Doxographi
Graeci* (Berlin, 1879) 547.

A theory of signs is never easy; an Epicurean one is made the more difficult by certain of its main tenets. Its atoms, for example, are distinguishable only by size, position, and shape; internally, they are all the same matter. They also are colorless, so that it would be wrong to infer that an atom of gold is golden in color. Epicureans also argued that "the things in this universe are as large as we see them to be" (col. 14, trans. De Lacy and De Lacy). How to infer the size of the sun, therefore, is a particular challenge to them, for it appears to be the size of a human foot, as the pre-Socratic philosopher Herakleitos once said (perhaps not seriously). Since, however, the sun seems not to lose its brilliance with distance, unlike other objects, it must be exceptional also in remaining the same (small) size, no matter how far away it is.

On Ethics

Philodemos wrote on ethics in an encyclopedic manner, dividing this broad and all-important subject into many individual books. The work as a whole has the cumbrous title *On Vices and Their Corresponding Virtues and Those in Whom They Are Present and about What They Concern.* The book divisions have more memorable titles: Book 1, *On Flattery;* Book 9, *On Household Management,*[167] and Book 10, which, although missing its title in the papyrus, is regularly called *On Arrogance.* PHerc. 253 and 1457, entitled simply *On Vices,* are reasonably taken to be yet other books.

Another work of Philodemos is usually called simply *On Anger,* but its full title, "Philodemos *On (Ethical) Character; That Is, On Anger,*" allows for the possibility that *On Anger* is part of a larger work, whose full title we have in *PHerc.* 1471, "Philodemos, *Epitome* [i.e., *Abridgement*] of *Zenon's Lectures on Conduct* [literally, *Lives*] *and Character; That Is, On Freedom of Speech.*" Other works having to do with virtues and vices are not specifically identified as coming from this large work; some, in fact, have no titles remaining at all, such as *PHerc.* 312, whose scraps mention marriage, on the basis of which it has been tentatively entitled *On Marriage.* (Agathe Antoni is preparing an edition.)

It should be noted that *On Marriage* is not a sociological study, *On Freedom of Speech* is not political, *On Wealth* is not a work of economy, *On Death* is not a work of biology, and *On Anger* is not a treatise that Freud would recognize as psychological (one could, though, say that it deals with anger management). These and other works are quite properly categorized as ethical, for they argue

rerum futurarum veritatem:
quorum nihil tale est, ut in eo
vis divina inesse videatur.

Et haec quidem in primo 41
5 libro De natura deorum, in
secundo autem volt Orphei,
Musaei, Hesiodi Homerique
fabellas accommodare ad ea,
quae ipse primo libro de
10 deis immortalibus dixerat,
ut etiam veterrimi poëtae, qui
haec ne suspicati quidem sunt,
Stoïci fuisse videantur.

ι τὸν πε)ρὶ τὴν (γῆ)ν ἀ-
έρα, (τ)ὸ⟨ν⟩ δὲ σκο(τει)νὸν
Ἄιδ(ην), τὸν δὲ διὰ τῆς
5 γῆ(ς κ)αὶ θαλάτ(τ)ης Πο-
σ(ειδῶ). καὶ το(ὺς) ἄλ-
λου(ς δ)ὲ θεοὺς ἀψύχοις
ὡς καὶ τούτους συν-
οικειοῖ· καὶ τὸν ἥλ(ι-
10 όν (τε) καὶ τὴ(ν) σελή-
νην καὶ τοὺς ἄλλους
ἀστέ(ρ)ας θεοὺς οἴε-
ται καὶ τὸν νόμον.
κα(ὶ ἀν)θρώπους εἰς
15 θεο(ύ)ς φησι με(τ)αβα-
λεῖ(ν). ἐν δὲ τῷ δευ-
τέ(ρῳ) τά τ(ε) εἰς Ὀρφέ-
α (καὶ Μ)ουσαῖον ἀνα-
φε(ρόμ)ε(ν)α καὶ (τ)ὰ
20 παρ' (Ὁ)μήρῳ καὶ Ἡ-
σιόδ(ῳ) καὶ Εὐρι(π)ί-
δη κ[ι]αὶ ποιηταῖς ἄλ-
λοις, (ὥ)ς κα(ὶ) Κλεάν-
θης, (π)ειρᾶτα(ι συ)νοι-
25 κειοῦ(ν) ταῖς δόξαις
αὐτῶ(ν). ἅπαντά (τ') ἐσ-
τὶν αἰθήρ, ὁ αὐ(τ)ὸς
ὢν καὶ πατὴρ καὶ
υἱός, (ὡς) κἂν τῷ
30 πρώτῳ μὴ μά-
χεσθαι τὸ τὴν Ῥέ-
c. 14 1 α)ν καὶ μητέρα (τοῦ   p. 81 G.
Διὸς εἶναι καὶ θ(υγα-
τέρα. τὰς δ' αὐτὰς
πο(ι)εῖται σ(υ)νοικει-
5 ώσε)ις κἂν τῷ Περὶ
Χ)αρίτων, (ἐν ᾧ τ)ὸν
Δία νόμον φησὶ⟨ν⟩ εἶ-
ναι καὶ τὰς Χάριτας
τὰς ἡμετέ(ρ)ας κα-

FIGURE 78

Memento mori ("remember that you are mortal"). This
mosaic tabletop from Pompeii contains several reminders of
mortality, including a skull, butterfly, wheel, and a carpenter's
balance, whose plumb line, crossing the horizontal bar at
right angles, shows that the skull (= death) equally balances
the poor man's sack (on the right) and the ruler's scepter (on
the left). Naples, Museo Archeologico Nazionale, inv. 109982.
See Otto J. Brendel, "Observations on the Allegory of the
Pompeian Death's-Head Mosaic," in his *The Visible Idea*
(Washington, D.C., 1980) 7–25.

90

the Epicurean case for when (if ever) the philosopher should marry, how and when to say what to
whom, how to maintain the proper disdain for the acquisition of money for its own sake, how to
live free of the fear of death, how to control and (when necessary) direct one's rage, etc.[168] Epicurean
ethics thus had something to say about all sorts of human actions and attitudes. Although Epikouros
himself, following up on the groundbreaking work of the pre-Socratic philosopher Demokritos,
built his ethical theory on atomic theory—he tried, in other (famous philosophical) words, to get
from *is* to *ought*—there is none of this in the ethical treatises found in the Villa, which take the physical, i.e., scientific, basis for granted.[169] (One can, however, see it in Lucretius's long poem.)

We can examine here only some examples of these tenets and prescriptions as they are found in the
works of Philodemos. *On Freedom of Speech* (*PHerc.* 1471) is particularly well preserved, and its empirical nature means that no important philosophical nuances have been lost.[170] The Greek title is *Parrhesia*,

which translates literally as "saying all" (from *pan*
+ *rhesis*); in its usual political and ethical usage it
can be unpacked to mean "to say all that one
thinks should be said," or "to speak one's mind."
Fifth- and fourth-century Athens was famous for
the free and frank speech of its citizens, and even
of its slaves, who frequently were as outspoken as
their masters. Non-Athenians were surprised by
this trait; nor did upper-class Athenians always
appreciate hearing what poorer citizens thought
of them. *Parrhesia* then came to have this sense
of frank criticism in the private sphere as well,
which is Philodemos's concern. There are times,
he argues, when *parrhesia* is called for; there are
also considerations that advise against its use. It
is wasted on kings, for example, who regard it as
insubordination. And "why is it that old men
grow annoyed by it? Because they think that time

has made them wiser and that people criticize them out of contempt" (col. 24a).[171]

Clearly, then, the teacher, the wise person, or the philosopher will direct his or her criticism where it will do the most good. A teacher will still have to exercize caution, but only through frank criticism can a student learn from his mistakes. Among Epicureans, on the other hand, *parrhesia* is a necessity. Indeed, it is a failing *not* to offer criticism to one's fellow Epicurean.[172] To put this point as strongly as possible, Philodemos wrote an epigram in which he cast himself as an imperfect Epicurean, one who bewails to his girlfriend Xantho the fact that he must some day die. He then has Xantho deliver a crushing example of *parrhesia,* reminding him of the Epicurean notion, not only that "death is nothing to us," but that weeping over it can only rob us of the pleasures that life has to offer:

Memento mori (*Anthologia Palatina* 9.570)

> *Man:* Xantho, did an artist mold you?
> Did your voice come from a bird?
> Sweet perfection, when I hold you
> "Goddess" is my only word.
> Someday I will sleep forever
> Lonely in the arms of death.
> Meanwhile, play me something clever,
> Xantho, while I still have breath.
> Longing for your playing lingers,
> Dewy songs from fragrant fingers:
> Yes, yes! That's the sweetest song!
> *Xantho:* Enough of singing! Come along!
> I think for two there'll be no room
> In your rocky, lonely tomb.[173]

It is not chance that led Philodemos here and in another, similary structured, parrhesiastic epigram to choose death as the subject, for dispelling the fear of death was considered one of the most important steps toward attaining *ataraxia,* an undisturbed state of mind, necessary for happiness. Indeed,

Epikouros made the phrase "death is nothing to us" one of his *tetrapharmakos*, his "four-part cure" for all that ails most of mankind.[174] This pithy and intentionally contemptuous phrase is familiar to readers of Lucretius in the form *mors nihil ad nos* (death is nothing to us). Strangely, however, when Philodemos quotes the *tetrapharmakos* in his *Against the* [. . .] col. 5.10–14 (*PHerc.* 1005; see p. 81), he paraphrases it feebly as "nothing expected in death," that is, "expect nothing in/from death" (FIGS. 78, 79, 80).

However Philodemos weakens Epikouros's tart phrase, dispelling the fear of death remains as important in his writings as in that of any Epicurean. Substantial portions remain among the papyri of the fourth book of Philodemos's *On Death* (*PHerc.* 1050), which seems to have been one of his more comprehensive works.[175] Death itself is simple, however: It is the dissolution of our material selves, including our equally material souls and minds. There would be, therefore, nothing left to perceive anything, let alone any discomfort or pain. The great length of the work, therefore, would have been devoted largely to describing the proper attitude to maintain in the face of our own mortality and that of the people close to us. Once again, Lucretius's account (at the end of Book 3) covers much of the same ground, in general and even in the closeness of some of his translations. Lucretius may also have been familiar with Philodemos's epigram on death, which was just quoted above. Thus, Philodemos's paradoxical phrase for death, "sleep a deathlessly long time," shows up in Lucretius as *mors immortalis*, "immortal death" (3.869).

On Poetic Theory

However important the discovery of Philodemos's library was and continues to be, it must be confessed that for the most part its major contribution has been to fill in the gaps left by the loss of so much of Epikouros's writings. Epikouros, however, was rather insensitive to literary criticism, even if the older view that he was actively hostile to poetry itself has largely been disproved.[176] As a practicing poet himself, and as a friend of many Roman poets, Philodemos was naturally drawn to thinking about the important elements of poetry. It could hardly be otherwise in an age when literary criticism flourished, first among Greeks in the Hellenistic period and then among the Roman poets who were their immediate heirs.[177] Philodemos spanned both worlds.[178]

Since, as we have seen, it was Philodemos's regular practice first to lay out the views of his opponents, his works on poetry give us (along with much of the usual difficulty of interpretation, it is true)

93

not only his own distinct and important views but also those of his Hellenistic predecessors, all of whose works have been lost. It is thanks only, or almost entirely, to Philodemos, therefore, that we now have a far better idea than ever before of the poetic theories of Krates of Mallos (who also wrote on Homer), Herakleodoros, Pausimakhos, Megakleides of Athens, Neoptolemos of Parion, and Andromenides. Apart from Krates, who was known for his work on the text of Homer, and Neoptolemos, whose theories were known to have been used by Horace in his *Ars poetica,* these critics are unknown to all but the most ardent students of Hellenistic literary criticism. Unknown to us, perhaps, but certainly known to Vergil and the other erudite poets of Rome, whose poetic programs often allude to the theories of their predecessors.[179]

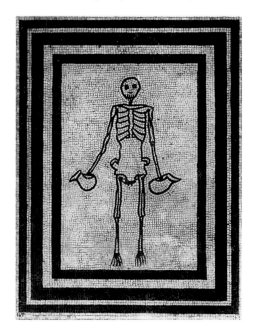

As an example of how crucial it can be to know the literary theories elliptically alluded to by poets, we can cite Philodemos's own poems. At least seven times in his epigrams, Philodemos names Xanthippe as his inamorata, either in full or by the nicknames Xantharion, Xanthion, or Xantho. Whether she represents a real woman in his life or is fictional, why did he choose this name? Since there is some evidence that Sokration ("little Sokrates") was a nickname for Philodemos (see p. 6), it would make sense for his woman (who in some poems seems to be his wife) to be given the name of the original Sokrates' wife (who was nowhere near as shrewish as some anti-Socratic literature makes out).[180]

There is, however, in addition to this "autobiographical" reason, an aesthetic one. In his prose treatise *On Poems,* Book 2, Philodemos attacks, among many others, those who make euphony the chief criterion by which to judge a poem's worth. Philodemos, a poet himself, is not deaf to the beauty of a poem's sound (especially since almost all poetry in the ancient world was meant to be recited), but he sees euphony as only one element of the successful poem. He would, moreover, rate a poem's "idea" as its most important element, one that could override all else. Thus, in one poem, with some insultingly rough language, he allows himself to violate some metrical norms that he is careful to observe elsewhere. In choosing the "ugly" name Xanthippe (which begins with the cacophonous *ks*-sound that the euphonists hated), he shows the euphonists ever so obliquely (which is the way Hellenistic poets liked to work) just how wrong-headed their theory is, for they had listed some names that they considered cacophonous: Phoinix, Zethos, and Xanth[ ], which could be restored as Xanth[os] or (as I like to think) as Philodemos's Xanth[o]. For Philodemos, then, the epigram, sometimes thought of as a lightweight genre, could demonstrate the excellence of poetry as well as the metrically elaborate lyrics of Sappho—which is in fact what he says in Book 5 of *On Poems* (col. 38.7–15).[181]

There is another poetic lesson to be learned here. Philodemos shared some of Epikouros's mistrust of Socratic values, but the idea of a poem is not to be held to the same standard of truth as a philosophical argument. Philodemos illustrated this in his epigrams, which draw freely from rival philosophical schools. In short—and this is his major contribution to literary criticism—art has its own standards of truth. As he puts it rather strikingly, even bad men can be skilled writers; even more famous is his dictum that "poems, insofar as they are poems, do not provide benefit." In the immortal words of Samuel Goldwyn, *ars gratia artis*.[182] Furthermore, not only did the worth of a poem not lie in its ability to benefit its readers, Philodemos argued elsewhere that poetry can never improve our lives; only well-argued philosophical prose can do that. The "idea" of a poem (*dianoia* in Greek) is most important, but, he argues, it does not matter whether the idea is right or true (which for Philodemos means in accord with Epicurean doctrine). For the poem to succeed as a poem, its idea must be expressed in accordance with the principles of aesthetics he details in his treatises.

How large was the Villa's library, and what was its full extent? This is impossible to say. Some good portion, along with some other portable household valuables, may have been carried away as the nature of the eruption became clear. A second, depressing possibility: Since the majority of the extant Latin papyri were found in but one *capsa*, and those authors who can be identified have names that begin the *C, E,*

FIGURE 80

One of two drinking cups from Boscoreale, depicting (and labeling) poets and philosophers, all shown as skeletons. Among the philosophers, facing each other, are the founders of the two leading Hellenistic philosophical schools: Zenon the Stoic and Epikouros, who reaches for some food and around whose legs a pig frolics. An inscription over the food reads, "The goal is pleasure." Another inscription reads, "Live life to the full, for tomorrow is uncertain," which Philodemos in his *On Death* exaggerated into, "It's not only tomorrow that is uncertain; so too is the present moment." Silver, H. 10.6 cm (4 1/8 in.). Paris, Musée du Louvre, inv. BJ 1923. Photo: Erich Lessing/Art Resource, NY.

and *L*, the Villa may have contained only the smallest collection of Latin texts, for we know from other sources that book owners then, as now, employed one or another ordering scheme. Thus, when Galen, in the second century A.D., lists some of the books lost in a fire, he gives the names Aristotle, Anaxagoras, and Andromachos; that is, it would seem, the books from his alpha *capsa* or shelf.[183]

There remains a third, and more hopeful, possibility—that the bulk of the Latin library remains to be found. Look at the plan for that part of the Villa where the Greek rolls were found (see FIG. 64). The peristyle would not have been built along the edge of the structure. Where the plan is now blank, there must have been rooms that today remain to be excavated. One of these may well contain a collection of texts—Greek, Latin, or both—that, when opened, could supplement and correct the relatively small number of extant works of classical (and preclassical) literature. These texts would, of course, be as carbonized as the ones we have described, but without the loss that the rolls initially suffered, and with the application of the latest techniques for unrolling and reading, we would, it is easy to imagine, have near contemporary texts of Lucretius and Vergil. Authors whose medieval manuscripts are in especially bad shape, such as the difficult elegiac poet Propertius, could be read as intended for the first time since antiquity. If all of Philodemos's library became part of the Villa's holdings, then lost texts of the lyric poets he quotes could have been separated from the philosophical section and shelved with other works of Greek literature. It is something to hope for.

APPENDIX 1
English Translations of Epikouros and Philodemos

EPIKOUROS

Cyril Bailey, *Epicurus: The Extant Remains* (Oxford, 1926; repr. Hildesheim, 1970). A standard trans. of the manuscript remains and of the important life of Epikouros in Diogenes Laertios, but containing nothing known from papyri.

Brad Inwood, L. P. Gerson, and D. S. Hutchinson, *The Epicurus Reader: Selected Writings and Testimonia* (Indianapolis, 1994). In addition to some valuable ancient secondary testimony that supplements what remains of Epikouros's writings, this book also contains a passage from Epikouros *On Nature,* Book 25, found in the Villa.

PHILODEMOS

On Choices and Avoidances

Giovanni Indelli and Voula Tsouna-McKirahan, [*Philodemus: On Choices and Avoidances.*] Naples, 1995. The brackets are to warn the reader that the papyrus does not name the author (Philodemos is likely) or title (ethical choices and avoidances are merely the subject of the extant columns).

Epigrams

David Sider, *The Epigrams of Philodemos* (New York, 1997).
Sandra Sider, "Philodemus," *Classical Outlook 61* (1984) 79–80. Trans. of six epigrams.

On Frank Criticism

David Konstan et al., *Philodemus on Frank Criticism,* Society of Biblical Literature, Texts and Translations, 43 (Atlanta, 1998). Introduction, trans., and notes.

Clarence Glad, in John T. Fitzgerald, ed., *Friendship, Flattery, and Frankness of Speech* (Leiden, 1995).

The Good King according to Homer

Elizabeth Asmis, "Philodemus' Poetic Theory and *On The Good King according to Homer,*" *Classical Antiquity* 10 (1991) 1–45. The trans. is on pp. 28–45.

Jeffrey Fish, "Philodemus' *On the Good King according to Homer: Columns 21–31,*" CErc 32 (2002) 187–234. A complete edition is forthcoming.

On Methods of Inference

Phillip Howard De Lacy and Estelle Allen De Lacy, *Philodemus: On Methods of Inference,* 2nd edn. (Naples, 1978).

Dirk Obbink, *Philodemus* On Piety. *Part 1: Critical Text with Commentary* (Oxford, 1996).
Dirk Obbink, *Philodemus* On Piety. *Part 2: Critical Text with Commentary* (Oxford, 2005).

On Poems

Book 1. Richard Janko, *Philodemus* On Poems, *Book 1* (Oxford, 2000).
Book 4. Richard Janko, "Philodemus's *On Poems* and Aristotle's *On Poets,*" *CErc* 21 (1991) 5–64.
Book 5. David Armstrong, in Dirk Obbink, ed., *Philodemus and Poetry: Poetic Theory and Practice in Lucretius, Philodemus, and Horace* (New York, 1995) 255–69.

On Rhetoric

Harry M. Hubbell, "The Rhetoric of Philodemus," *Transactions of the Connecticut Academy of Arts and Sciences* 23 (1920) 243–382. Trans. and commentary. Hubbell's translation can stand, but the structure of the *Rhetoric* has been improved by later scholars.

C. E. Chandler, *Philodemus* On Rhetoric, *Books 1 and 2: Translation and Exegetical Essays,* Ph.D. diss. (University of Cape Town, 2000).

Forthcoming are trans. of *On Poems,* Books 2–5, *On Rhetoric,* and *On Music,* all in the Philodemus Translation Series, Oxford.

Publication of the Herculaneum papyri began in 1793 with Philodemos's *On Music* 4, in the series *Herculanensium Voluminum quae supersunt* (*HV*); a total of eleven volumes were published in Naples, the last one in 1855. In all, nineteen texts were published, which, although not in itself an impressive number, was enough to alert scholars and humanists all over Europe to the scope and importance of the finds. These volumes were beautifully printed on large-scale pages, and the engravings were printed in two colors, black for the legible text, red for conjectural fillings of the lacunae (see FIGS. 56, 57).

To meet the call for faster publication, a more modest *Collectio altera* was started in 1862. This series, too, attained eleven volumes before ceasing in 1876, but because it largely reproduced the *disegni*, without the time-consuming editorial care given to the texts, it included 162 rolls. A projected *Collectio tertia,* the first to include photographs of the papyri, managed only one volume, in 1914, and did not continue after the war.

Fortunately, a series that was designed for the pocketbooks of the ordinary scholar, the Bibliotheca Teubneriana, published in Leipzig, had begun to include Philodemos, first in 1892, with Siegfried Sudhaus's still-magisterial and indispensible three-volume edition of the *Rhetoric.* All told, the series published seven works of Philodemos and one of Polystratos, the last ones in 1914. This series, some volumes of which are still standard texts, however, merely represents one part of the extended interest in the papyri manifested by German scholars that began with Theodor Gomperz's edition of *On Anger* in 1864 and Franz Büchler's edition of *On Piety* in 1865. See Marcello Gigante's excellent survey of the German contribution to the publication of these texts: *La Germania e i papiri ercolanesi* (Heidelberg, 1988).

Other important titles were Hermann Diels's editions of Philodemos *On the Gods* 1 (1906) and 3 (1917) and Christian Jensen's of Philodemos *On Poetry* 5 (1923), which for many decades whetted the interest of all students of ancient literary criticism with its intriguing but partial (in both senses of the word) accounts of now-lost literary theories from the time of and just before Philodemos. (See pp. 93ff.)

Another series dedicated to the Herculaneum papyri was started by Marcello Gigante, the scholar who almost single-handedly revived flagging interest in the the papyri: *La Scuola di Epicuro,* the first volume of which was published in 1978; the series continues to this day. Before Gigante, access to the papyri had been difficult at best, and for foreigners all but impossible. As head of the Officina dei Papiri in Naples, in contrast, Gigante actively invited the participation of all scholars who had the patience and the necessary philological skills. Texts published earlier were reedited (for example, *On Music* 4 and *On the Good King according to Homer*), and as new papyri were unrolled (an effort also strongly supported by Gigante), texts were published for the first time, if not in *La Scuola di Epicuro,* then in the journal he inaugurated together with other Italian scholars in 1971, *Cronache Ercolanesi* (*CErc*), whose very first article issued a call to scholars: Eric Turner (a well-known British papyrologist), "The Need for New Work on the Papyri from Herculaneum." *CErc,* moreover, does not limit itself to the papyri, but has over the years published many important articles on all the finds from Herculaneum, including its graffiti, mosaics, wall-paintings, and architecture. It has also published many articles on the history of the Officina dei Papiri and the many early figures

responsible for discovering, preserving, reading, and publishing; the authors of these articles typically rediscover important but neglected letters and other documents in the various Neapolitan
archives. (Many of these, but by no means all, have been cited here.)

More recently, thanks to initial and generous support from the National Endowment for the
Humanities, a program has been undertaken to publish editions with translations of all of Philodemos's aesthetic works, that is, his works on poetry, rhetoric, and music. Dirk Obbink's edition of
the second part of Philodemos's *On Piety* could almost be included in this group, since it is here
that Philodemos discusses the way in which poets mention the gods.

This has been but a brief survey of the publishing history of the papyri. Far fuller information is
provided by the *Catalogo dei papiri ercolanesi,* edited by Marcello Gigante, with its two supplements
(see annotated bibliography, p. 116), arranged by *PHerc.* numbers. For a less complete but still useful
source of publications of Philodemos and other Epicureans, arranged alphabetically by author, see
Luci Berkowitz and Karl A. Squitier, *Thesaurus Linguae Graecae: Canon of Greek Authors,* 3rd edn.
(New York, 1990).

For more on the publishing history of the papyri, see Francesca Longo Auricchio, "La Villa
Ercolanese dei Papiri: Storia delle scoperte e vita dell'Officina [dei Papiri] dal Museo di Portici al
Palazzo Reale di Napoli," *CErc* 30 (2000) 11–20. *HV* were published by La Stamperia Reale di Napoli,
on which press see Maria Gabriella Mansi and Agnese Travaglione, *La Stamperia Reale di Napoli,*
1748–1860. I Quaderni della Biblioteca Nazionale di Napoli, Ser. 9.3 (Naples, 2002).

Notes

1. For the fullest account of ownership of the Villa, see Mario Capasso, *Manuale di papirologia ercolanese* (Galatina, 1991) 43–64.

    Roman males usually had three names: (i) a *praenomen,* equivalent to our first name (e.g., Gaius, Lucius, Titus); (ii) a *nomen,* in the form of an adjective to denote the (extended) family, or *gens* (e.g., Julius, Claudius, Calpurnius); (iii) and a *cognomen,* to identify a branch of the *gens* (e.g., Piso); they might also have (iv) an additional *cognomen* to provide further distinction within the family (e.g., Caesoninus, Pontifex). Women tended to be identified solely by *nomen* so that any and all daughters born into the *gens Calpurnia* had to be named Calpurnia.

2. See Carol C. Mattusch, *The Villa dei Papiri at Herculaneum: Life and Afterlife of a Sculpture Collection* (Los Angeles, 2005).

3. *Anthologia Palatina* 11.44 = Philodemos *Epigram* 27.

4. Catullus 47, which begins *Porci et Socration, duae sinistrae | Pisonis,* "Porcius and Socration, two left-hands of Piso." It is by no means certain, however, which member of the Piso family is addressed here, nor who Porcius and Socration really are. Nicknames were common among friends, and "Porcius" looks like yet another reference to Epicurean pigs (see FIGS. 2, 80).

5. On the other hand, it must be noted that all the texts have been written by professional scribes; that is, they may have been published. It thus is possible, although this is a minority view, that the first-century-B.C. owner of the Villa dei Papiri (who need not have been Piso) collected, along with much else, the words of the most famous Epicurean working on the Bay of Naples.

6. That is, *Papyrus Herculanensis.* The numbers were first given by Antonio Piaggio (see p. 22), and are still being added to today. Some few Herculaneum papyri were taken to Paris and thus have been given *PHerc.Paris* numbers, such as the extremely important fragment that has Philodemos addressing Vergil. See Richard Janko, *Philodemos On Poems, Book 1* (2000; rev. edn. Oxford, 2003).

7. Theodor Mommsen, "Inschriftbüsten I. Aus Herculaneum," *Archäologische Zeitung* 38 (1880) 32–36. Agreeing with Mommsen were his German contemporaries but not the Italians, who, perhaps for sentimental reasons, championed Piso.

8. On Piso's travels in Greece and his philhellenism, see Herbert Bloch, "L. Calpurnius Piso Caesoninus in Samothrace and Herculaneum," *American Journal of Archaeology* 44 (1940) 485–93, who argues for Piso's being the owner of the Villa. Philhellenism, however, was endemic among upper-class Romans, who could not be considered educated without a thorough grounding in Greek literature, as Cicero himself says in his speech *Pro Archia.*

9. Dimitrios Pandermalis, "Zum Programm der Statuenausstattung in der Villa dei Papiri," *Mitteilungen des Deutschen Archäologischen Instituts, Athenische Abteilung* 86 (1971) 173–209.

10. Antipater of Thessalonika 31: A. S. F. Gow and D. L. Page, eds., *The Greek Anthology: The Garland of Philip* (Cambridge, 1968) 9.93. The other poems addressed to Piso are 1, 30, and 40–45.

11. It should also be said that the attempts to identify a bust found somewhere else in Herculaneum as that of Piso Frugi are not convincing. See Stefania Adamo Muscettola, "Il ritratto di Lucio Calpurnio Pisone Pontefice da Ercolano," *CErc* 20 (1990) 145–55. (See FIG. 4.)

12. The strongest partisan of Claudius, who is surely the best candidate for owner after Piso, is Maria Rita Wojcik, *La Villa dei Papiri ad Ercolano: Contributo alla ricostruzione dell'ideologia della nobilitas tardorepubblicana* (Rome, 1986) 276–84.

13. Walter Allen and Phillip De Lacy, "The Patrons of Philodemos," *Classical Philology* 34 (1939) 59–65.

14. See Marcello Gigante, *Philodemus in Italy: The Books from Herculaneum,* trans. Dirk Obbink (Ann Arbor, 2002) 54–59. For a detailed argument against Gigante's view, see David Sider, *The Epigrams of Philodemos* (New York, 1997) 167f.

15. A nonscientist, I am happy to send the reader to my sources for much of this ch.: Haraldur Sigurdsson, Stanford Cashdollar, and S. R. J. Sparks, "The Eruption of Vesuvius in A.D. 79: Reconstruction from Historical and Volcanological Evidence," *American Journal of Archaeology* 86 (1982) 39–51; Haraldur Sigurdsson, "Mount Vesuvius before the Disaster," and Haraldur Sigurdsson and Steven Carey, "The Eruption of Vesuvius in A.D. 79," both in Wilhelmina F. Jashemski and Frederick G. Meyer, eds., *A Natural History of Pompeii* (Cambridge, 2002), chs. 3 and 4. Indeed, this entire volume is to be recommended for its chs. on the flora and fauna of the Naples area, as well as one on the human remains of the eruption. The literary sources for the area and the eruption are treated at greater length in Marcello Gigante, *Il Fungo sul Vesuvio secondo Plinio il Giovane* (Rome, 1989); and Ernesto De Carolis and Giovanni Patricelli, *Vesuvius A.D. 79: The Destruction of Pompeii and Herculaneum* (Los Angeles, 2003), which reproduces many archival photographs of nineteenth-century excavations.

16. On 8 January 1944, there was a preliminary eruption of lava: Two streams converged about four hundred feet below the summit, producing what some Italians took to be a V-sign portending imminent Allied victory in the war. On 19 March, while the *New York Times* front-page headline announced that "Nazis Hit back on

Cassino's Rim," further south, where the U.S. Army was now in control, "Vesuvius Erupts in Violent Action," with lava flows of 35–40 miles per hour and temperatures of 2,500 degrees. The town of San Sebastiano was destroyed. An American corporal was quoted as saying "Gosh, wait when I tell 'em about this in Muncie."

17. Seneca in this section also describes a situation very much like that in Vergil, where sheep near Pompeii died from breathing air "tainted by the poison of the fires beneath the earth," which did not affect people, whose faces were higher off the ground. Similarly, Sigurdsson, "Vesuvius before the Disaster" (see n. 15) 35 describes the death of sheep in a volcanic area of Iceland, and, on an island south of Iceland, the death of sparrows in a layer of carbon dioxide thin enough to spare seagulls.

18. Pliny's letters date from A.D. 106 or 107. Unfortunately the part of Tacitus's history that covered the eruption has been lost.

19. In full, the uncle was Gaius Plinius Secundus, the nephew Gaius Plinius Caecilius Secundus. For an account of the Elder Pliny's encyclopedic *Natural History,* see Roger French, *Ancient Natural History* (London and New York, 1994) 196–255. Both Plinys are available in English trans. in the Loeb Classical Library (Harvard Univ. Press).

20. *Pinus pinea,* common throughout the Mediterranean and the source of pignoli, which the Romans used in salads, sausages, and desserts. See Oleg Polunin, *Trees and Bushes of Britain and Europe* (London, 1976); and Jashemski and Meyer (see n. 15) 143–44, with an illustration from a Pompeian wall-painting, fig. 127. Nowadays we call a smoke cloud of this shape a mushroom cloud.

21. Excerpted and paraphrased from Pliny *Letters* 6.16. Pliny the Younger was seventeen in A.D. 79.

22. Martial 4.44. Nysa and Lakedaimon (Sparta) were the sites of famous temples to, respectively, Bacchus (Dionysos) and Venus (Aphrodite), who was also the patron deity of Pompeii. Hercules (Herakles) was said to have founded Herculaneum after fighting against a race of Giants in the fields near Cumae, which "had been named Phlegraean in honor of the peak that in the past had breathed forth fire, very much like Sicilian Etna. The peak, now called Vesuvius, shows many signs of having been burned in the distant past" (Diodoros of Sicily 4.21.5). These Giants, like the Kyklopes, Typhoeus, and other monsters, were mighty creatures frequently associated with volcanoes and earthquakes. Note also that Martial calls the mountain *Vesbius,* which, like *Vesvius,* was a variant; and any variant with a different metrical scheme would be kept alive by the poets.

23. Statius *Silvae* 5.5.72–74. For his other references to Vesuvius, during and after the eruption, see 2.6.61f., 4.4.78–85, 4.8.5, 5.3.104–6, 5.3.164f., 5.3.205–8. Gigante,

Il Fungo sul Vesuvio (see n. 15) 15–17, discusses them all.

24. The new town was called Resina until 1967, when, in honor of its ancient predecessor, it was renamed Ercolano.

25. Joseph Jay Deiss, *Herculaneum: Italy's Buried Treasure* (Malibu, CA, 1989) 35. In this ch. I am indebted also to Christopher Parslow, *Rediscovering Antiquity: Karl Weber and the Excavation of Herculaneum, Pompeii, and Stabiae* (Cambridge, 1995); Charles Waldstein and Leonard Shoobridge, *Herculaneum: Past, Present, and Future* (London, 1908); and Mattusch, *The Villa dei Papiri at Herculaneum* (see n. 2).

26. Johann Joachim Winckelmann, *Critical Account of the Situation and Destruction by the First Eruptions of Mount Vesuvius of Herculaneum, Pompeii, and Stabia . . .* (London, 1771), 22. See Francesca Longo Auricchio, "Le prime scoperte a Ercolano," *CErc* 27 (1997) 175–79. On the marbles, see Valerio Papaccio, *Marmi ercolanesi in Francia* (Naples, 1995).

27. This and all of Paderni's reports, along with other excavation reports, were reprinted in Domenico Comparetti and Giulio De Petra, *La Villa ercolanese dei Pisoni: I suoi monumenti e la sua biblioteca* (1883; repr. Naples, 1972). For Paderni, see pp. 238–50. Other reports, unknown to Comparetti and De Petra, have been discovered in the archives in recent decades and have been made use of by Parslow, *Rediscovering Antiquity* (see n. 25). See also Mario Capasso, ed., *Bicentenario della morte di Antonio Piaggio: Raccolta di Studi = Papyrologica Lupiensia* 5 (Galatina, 1997), esp. M. G. Mansi, "Per un profilo di Camillo Paderni," pp. 77–108.

The Latin papyrus quoted by Paderni has since been lost. I suspect that it came from the *Carmen de Bello Actiaco* (see pp. 66f.), since the meter is consistent with dactylic hexameter, the words ("sweet," "cares," "cruel") would be appropriate, and the preserved fragments of this poem are ca. eight lines long.

28. The Neapolitan palm, which consisted of twelve *onzas,* equaled 26.46 cm (10 1/2 in.).

29. Comparetti and De Petra's (see n. 27) footnote here: "Forse qui si fa bello dell'opera del Piaggi!"; i.e., Paderni is taking credit for what was due to Piaggio.

30. From a document in Società Napoletana di Storia Patria (Naples). The story is well told by Parslow, *Rediscovering Antiquity* (see n. 25) 103–6, whose trans. of Piaggio I use. See further Francesca Longo Auricchio and Mario Capasso, "Nuove accessioni al *dossier* Piaggio," in *Contributi alla storia della Officina dei Papiri Ercolanesi.* I Quaderni della Biblioteca Nazionale di Napoli, Series V 2. I Papiri Ercolanesi III (Naples, 1980) 15–59; they review Piaggio's work and reprint many of his letters.

31. Trans. David Blank. See further below and David Blank, "Reflections on Re-reading Piaggio and the Early History of the Herculaneum Papyri," *CErc* 29 (1989) 55–82, esp.

p. 57, for this accusation made by Paderni (as recounted by Piaggio).

32. This list accounts for the vast majority of ancient writing. Note also the tale told by Herodotos of the tyrant Histiaios, who patiently passed on a secret message by tattooing it on the shaved head of a slave and then waiting for his hair to grow back before sending him on (Herodotos *Histories* 5.35.3). For this and some other exceptional forms of writing, see Deborah Tarn Steiner, *The Tyrant's Writ: Myth and Images of Writing in Ancient Greece* (Princeton, 1994) 3 n. 2.

    The famous writings on the walls of Herculaneum and Pompeii were either painted on (dipinti) or inscribed (graffiti); for selections with facsimiles and vocabulary notes, see Rex E. Wallace, *An Introduction to Wall Inscriptions from Pompeii and Herculaneum* (Wauconda, IL, 2005).

33. These were found not in the Villa dei Papiri but in the Casa del Scello di Legno (insula V, 31, which is identified on many tourist maps of Herculaneum). "Documentary" means "not literary," a term that in this context includes philosophy, history, etc. See Giuseppe Camodeca and Gianluca Del Mastro, "I papiri documentari ercolanesi (*PHerc.MAN*): Relazione preliminare," *CErc* 32 (2002) 281–96. For the tablets, with traces of wax remaining, which were found in Herculaneum, see Mario Capasso, "Le tavolette della Villa Ercolanese dei Papiri," in his *Volumen: Aspetti della tipologia del rotolo librario antico* (Naples, 1995) 111–17.

34. Euripides *Pleisthenes* fr. 627 Nauck-Kannicht.

35. The Hellenistic epigrammatist Poseidippos in one of his poems expresses the wish to be immortalized by a statue of himself reading from his own works.

36. The earlier spelling was *byblos,* named after the Phoenician city of Byblos (now Jubaye in Lebanon), which ancient sources tell us was the main port whence (Egyptian) papyrus was shipped to Greece. Similarly, parchment, made from animal skins, gets it name from the city of Pergamon; compare mocha and java as synonyms for coffee named after major exporting cities. By classical times, the word *byblion/biblion* had lost its diminutive force and become the standard word for "book." In the first century B.C. Philodemos still felt free to use the early form *bybl-*. See E. Puglia, "Βυβλοϛ e βυβλιον in Filodemo," *CErc* 16 (1986) 119–21. The Romans used the word *volumen* (which translates literally as "roll"; plural *volumina*). See also Mario Capasso, "Χάρτηϛ/*charta:* Primo contributo alla terminologia libraria antica," in his *Volumen* (see n. 33) 21–30.

37. See the ch. titled "La Persistance du rouleau," in Bernard Legras, *Lire en Égypte d'Alexandre à l'Islam* (Paris, 2002) 155–57—persistence, that is, in the face of the near universal domination of the codex format of the modern printed book, which has the two great advantages of allowing the reader to find any page with far greater speed than a scroll does, and of permitting both sides of its protected surfaces to be written on. E-books, on the other hand, return us to the practice of scrolling, at least virtually, through a text. For an account of how the codex quickly gained acceptance in the ancient world, in large part because the "Good Book" was spread through Europe in codex form, see Colin H. Roberts and T. C. Skeat, *The Birth of the Codex* (Oxford, 1983).

38. Trans. Arthur Hort in Loeb Classical Library. On the plant in general, see Naphtali Lewis, *Papyrus in Classical Antiquity* (Oxford, 1974). One cubit = 43–56 cm (17–22 in.).

39. Lucretius *On the Nature of Things* 6.114f. In the previous line Lucretius also likens the sound of papyrus being torn to thunder.

40. The papyrus plant was used in the manufacture of many other objects. The root was used for fuel; the fibers of the stalk were used to weave ropes, baskets, sails, clothing, and even entire boats. In addition, the stalk, especially its lower half, is slightly sweet and can be gnawed for the sugar, as my cat knows all too well, or used in stews and other dishes.

41. In the middle ages, animal skins, which were then used as writing surfaces, were often "smoothed/scraped again" (*palimpsest* in Greek) in order to reuse the surface for another text. Typically a pagan text was obliterated to make way for a Christian one. (There are far fewer papyrus palimpsests, since papyrus was both cheaper and more fragile than parchment.)

42. See Mario Capasso, "*Kollema* e *kollesis:* Per l'anatomia del rotolo ercolanese," in his *Volumen* (see n. 33) 55–71.

43. See my article "Pliny on the Manufacture of Paste for Papyrus," *ZPE* 22 (1976) 74.

44. Here are some lengths of *PHerc.* rolls: *On Music,* Book 4, 11.25 m (12.3 yds.); *On Poems,* Book 1, 16 m (17.5 yds., at least); and *On Piety,* 22.85 m (25 yds.). See Richard Janko, "The Herculaneum Library: Some Recent Developments," *Estudios Clásicos* 121 (2002) 25–41 (dimensions on pp. 27f.). Perhaps these figures should be increased, as it has been determined that papyri shrink when carbonized. On the length of papyrus rolls in general, see William A. Johnson, *Bookrolls and Scribes in Oxyrhynchus* (Toronto, 2004) 143–52, 217–30, who calculates lengths as much as 29 m (32 yds.—for Herodotos Book 7).

45. Or almost always on one side. There were occasions when, often because paper was scarce, the outside of the roll was written on as well.

46. See Mario Capasso, "Ὀμφαλοϛ/*umbilicus:* Dalla Grecia a Roma," in his *Volumen* (see n. 33) 73–98. *Omphalos* is the Greek word for "navel."

47. See Tiziano Dorandi, "Sillyboi," *Scrittura e Civiltà* 8 (1984) 185–99.

48. See F. C. Störmer et al., "Ink in Herculaneum," *CErc* 20 (1990) 183; and for ancient ink in general (some based on iron and oak-gall, others on squid ink), R. J. Forbes, *Studies in Ancient Technology* (Leiden, 1965) 3: 236–39. The ancient recipes are supplied by Pliny *Natural History* 35.25; Vitruvius *De Architectura* 7.10.2–4; and Dioskourides 5.182.
49. Nowadays we call an end-title a colophon, which is in fact a classical Greek word meaning "summit." Thus Plato could use the word metaphorically as the completion or final touch to an argument or discussion; that is, the colophon is part of the text itself. The sense of end-title is postclassical.
50. See Mario Capasso, "I titoli nei papiri ercolanesi. I. Un nuovo esempio di doppia soscrizione nel *PHerc.* 1675," in Mario Capasso, ed., *Il rotolo librario: Fabbricazione, restauro, organizzazione interna* (Galatina, 1994) = *Papyrologica Lupiensia* 3 (1994) 235–52; repr. in his *Volumen* (see n. 33) 119–37.
51. Eric G. Turner, *Greek Manuscripts of the Ancient World* (Princeton, 1971) 8. This and the other books by Turner in the bibl. offer excellent introductions to papyrus and papyrology.
52. See Enzo Puglia, "Dati bibliologici del *PHerc.* 1414," *CErc* 20 (1990) 61–64. Any and all such numbers, whether alongside the text or as totals at the end, are of obvious use to the editor of a papyrus text. See, e.g., Dirk Obbink, *Philodemus* On Piety. *Part 1: Critical Text with Commentary* (Oxford, 1996) 62–73.
53. Later, Alexandrian scholars developed an elaborate set of marginal signs to indicate their editorial views about textual questions. Thus, Aristarkhos, the Alexandrian Hellenistic scholar well known for his editions of Homer, Pindar, Aristophanes, et al., used the Greek letter chi (χ) simply to call the reader's attention to one or another unusual feature on the line marked. The *diplé* (>) alongside a line was similarly used to note a point of interest. The reader, thus alerted, would either see immediately what was being pointed out or would be expected to have access to a learned commentary (such as the ones written by Aristarkhos), which would spell it out.

Many other signs were added to texts, usually with quite specific editorial meanings. For example, the *obelos* (/), which was perhaps the first lectional sign used by the Alexandrian scholars, marked lines thought suspicious for one reason or another. The *obelos* as marginal sign derives from the word's original meaning: not the obol, a small coin, but from its earlier meaning of "spit" or "nail," which the sign roughly resembles. Editors of texts still use the term "obelize" to indicate a passage "damned" as not genuine. Soon a sizable roster of signs was developed. Another scholar, Zenodotos, employed the *asteriskos* (※) to designate Homeric lines repeated from another Homeric passage but there used (in Zenodotos's view) more appropriately. He used two other signs, the (lunate) sigma and the antisigma (Ϲ, Ͻ), to note two consecutive lines, only one of which (again, in his view) was necessary for the sense. The best study of papyrological lectional signs is Kathleen McNamee, "Abbreviations in Greek Literary Papyri and Ostraca," *Bulletin of the American Society of Papyrologists*, suppl. 3 (Chico, CA, 1981).

Scribes did not put spaces between words and, in our terms, all letters were capitals. THISDOESNOTMATT ERWHENREADINGPROSEANDTHEVOCABULARY ISFAMILIAR, but rarer words in archaic syntax such as WERETAUGHTTOMEIBORETHECANOPY would slow a reader down ("Were't aught to me I bore the canopy," Shakespeare, *Sonnet* 125.1.) There were occasions when an ancient scribe helped out the readers by punctuating in various ways. In some stone inscriptions as well as in some papyri or medieval manuscripts a raised dot or some other mark (such as a comma) would be placed between every word; or, if not between every word, then to prevent misdivision. Thus, in the sentence from Shakespeare's *Sonnet*, the equivalent aid would be WERE,T,AUGHT . . . , to ensure that "taught" was not read. Punctuation for sense existed by the fourth century B.C., even if it was rarely employed. When Herakleitos, a pre-Socratic philosopher notorious for his ambiguous prose, placed the word "always" in such a way that it could refer to either the preceding or the following word, Aristotle expressed disapproval that one could not readily *punctuate* the sentence (*diastixai*, i.e., put a point, *stigma*, between, *dia*) and place "always" with its proper reference. An English attempt to maintain Herakleitos's intentional ambiguity: "Of the *logos* that is always are men unaware" (Herakleitos fr. B 1 Diels-Kranz, quoted by Aristotle, *Rhetoric* 3.1409b18). Since, moreover, Herakleitos wrote well before accents and breathing marks were invented to aid the reader to distinguish between otherwise similar words, in another fr. (B 48) he uses the word *bios* in such a way that at first the reader pronounces it *biós*, "bow," but must by the end of the sentence recast it as *bíos*, "life." Modern editions of Herakleitos thwart his intention by printing *bíos*. In other words, Herakleitos, in the sixth century B.C., was the first Greek author to write for private *readers* rather than, as was the norm, for an audience of listeners. In support of this is the story that he deposited his work for safekeeping in the temple of Artemis in Ephesos, so that, we may imagine, if, as in fact proved to be the case, later writers were to garble his words (even by so little as supplying an unwanted comma), his original text would always remain as a kind of gold standard. Alas, the Temple of Artemis is now but a soggy hole in the ground, and scholars are forced to think in two ways at once in order to reinstate Herakleitos's original text. Cf. what Plutarch tells about the fourth-century orator Lykourgos, who had the texts of Aiskhylos, Sophokles, and Euripides kept on deposit in a public building in the Athenian Agora as copy texts for later productions, from which directors and actors were forbidden to deviate. In general, Aristotle says, the reader should be guided, "not by the scribe or by the *paragraphos,* but by the rhythm of the clause"; that is, by the author, whose prose style and rhythm leads the reader to a correct understanding of the text.

54. Our source for Pliny's studious habits is a letter written by his nephew, also called Pliny, where we learn that the Elder Pliny thought that "there was no book so bad that it was totally without profit," and that "every minute not given over to study was lost for ever" (Pliny, *Letters* 3.5). Nor was Pliny a passive listener. While one slave read, Pliny would indicate to another what passages to transcribe for eventual use in his own books. See Tiziano Dorandi, *Le Style et la tablette dans le secret des auteurs antiques* (Paris, 2000) 27–50.

55. Classical artists often name mythical figures and themselves on vases, but there are also many examples of completely nonsensical strings of letters. On this Sappho vase they are, in English equivalents, DINLNTTIN. See Henry R. Immerwahr, "Book Rolls on Attic Vases," in Charles Henderson, Jr., ed., *Classical, Mediaeval, and Renaissance Studies in Honor of Berthold Louis Ullman* (Rome, 1964) 1: 26, 46–47. Immerwahr should also be consulted for the two other vases with writing discussed immediately below.

56. See further Susan Guettel Cole, "Could Greek Women Read and Write?" in Helene P. Foley, ed., *Reflections of Women in Antiquity* (Philadelphia, 1981) 219–45.

57. Two modern depictions of ancient books perpetuate two of the errors discussed above, writing turned sideways and the ∫-curve: (i) A Greek stamp issued in 1996 shows a scroll with Homer's *Iliad* 8.436–45 clearly legible (illustrated in Legras, *Lire en Égypte* [see n. 37] pl. xvii); (ii) A *New Yorker* cartoon by Danny Shanahan shows an ancient homeowner unhappily reading a document that was just handed to him by, as the subtitle has it, "Hermes, process server of the gods." (24 October 1988; illustrated on the site www.cartoonbank.com; search under "Hermes.")

58. What follows is merely a sketch of the effect writing and books had upon the Greeks. For more complex accounts, see the essays of Eric A. Havelock in *The Literate Revolution in Greece and Its Cultural Consequences* (Princeton, 1982).

59. *Prometheus Bound* 460f. Although few classical scholars today believe that this play was written by Aiskhylos, its

fifth-century date seems secure.

60. Euripides *Palamedes* fr. 578 Nauck-Kannicht. For an account of the myth of Palamedes, see J. Platthy, *Sources on the Earliest Greek Libraries* (Amsterdam, 1968) 1–23.

61. See Hermann S. Schibli, *Pherekydes of Syros* (Oxford, 1990).

62. The trans. are taken from the excellent new (2000) Penguin trans. of *The Epic of Gilgamesh* by Andrew George.

63. For the ancient sources, see Plutarch *Sulla* 26 and Strabo *Geography* 13.1.851–53; for modern, more skeptical, accounts, R. G. Tanner, "Aristotle's Works: The Possible Origins of the Alexandria Collection," in Roy MacLeod, ed., *The Library of Alexandria: Centre of Learning in the Ancient World* (London, 2002) 79–91; F. Grayeff, *Aristotle and His School* (London, 1974), ch. 4, "The Library of the Peripatos and Its History."

64. Ioannes Tzetzes *Chiliades* 7.963–65.

65. Muses were often invoked at the beginning of literary works in a reverential way, most notably at the beginnings of the *Iliad* and *Odyssey*. Statues of the Muses would also have adorned any Mouseion; cf. Diogenes Laertios *Life of Theophrastos* 51, where Theophrastos sets aside funds for the repair of the statues in a Mouseion in Athens, which had suffered damaged during warfare. (He also designated funds to restore the maps painted in a nearby stoa.) There may even have been ceremonies during which prayers were offered to the Muses of the Mouseion, which was located in the Brucheion district of Alexandria, not far from the Jewish Quarter.

66. Diogenes Laertios *Life of Theophrastos* 5.52–53.

67. The second-most famous story of trans. in the ancient world is told by Pliny *Natural History* 18.22–23: Although Rome hated Carthage so much that it planned to raze the entire city, the Romans spared all the books, distributing them to the nearby rulers, with the exception of the large work on agriculture written in Phoenician, which, by decree of the Roman Senate, was translated into Latin.

68. See Plutarch *Life of the Ten Orators* 841f.; Galen *Commentary on Hippocrates' Epidemics III* (Berlin, 1955) 239–40, ed. Ernst August Wenkebach.

69. Very thorough studies of their editorial and exegetical work can be found in Rudolf Pfeiffer, *History of Classical Scholarship, from the Beginnings to the End of the Hellenistic Age* (Oxford, 1968); P. M. Fraser, *Ptolemaic Alexandria* (Oxford, 1972), esp. ch. 8, "Alexandrian Scholarship." On the subject of commentaries on classical texts in general, as established in antiquity and still produced today, see Glenn W. Most, ed., *Commentaries— Kommentare* (Göttingen, 1999); and Roy K. Gibson and Christina Shuttleworth Kraus, eds., *The Classical Commentary: Histories, Practices, Theory* (Leiden, 2002).

70. On the destruction of the library, see Robert Barnes,

"Cloistered Bookworms in the Chicken-coop of the Muses: The Ancient Library of Alexandria," in MacLeod, *The Library of Alexandria* (see n. 63), 61–77, esp. 70–74. The phrase "chicken-coop of the Muses" comes from Timon.

71. See Rudolf Blum, *Kallimachos: The Alexandrian Library and the Origins of Bibliography*, trans. H. H. Wellisch (Madison, 1991).

72. As part of his introduction to his book on Kallimakhos's *Hymn to Delos,* Bing gives the best account of how enthusiastically Hellenistic poets embraced and acknowledged the physicality of their writings: Peter Bing, *The Well-Read Muse: Present and Past in Callimachus and the Hellenistic Poets* (Göttingen, 1988) 10–48.

73. J. M. Jacques, "Sur un acrostiche d'Aratos (*Phén.* 783–87)," *Revue des Études Anciennes* 62 (1960) 48–61. Since then other Greek and Latin acrostics have been detected; see Edward Courtney, "Greek and Latin Acrostichs," *Philologus* 134 (1990) 3–13; Michael Haslam, "Hidden Signs: Aratus *Diosemeiai* 46ff., Vergil *Georgics* 1.424ff.," *Harvard Studies in Classical Philology* 94 (1992) 199–204.

74. *Epigram* 4 Sider.

75. Meleager *Epigram* 129, Gow-Page = *Anthologia Palatina* 12.257. See further T. C. Skeat, "The Use of Dictation in Ancient Book-Production," *Proceedings of the British Academy* 42 (1956) 183.

76. Philodemos *On Death* col. 39.18; Horace *Epistles* 1.16.79, which, since this is the last line of the book, would have had a line drawn under it. For further examples of metaphors in Philodemos, drawn from books, see Obbink, *Philodemus* On Piety (see n. 52) 88–93.

77. Trans. H. W. Fowler and F. G. Fowler, *The Works of Lucian of Samosata* (Oxford, 1905) 3: 265–78.

78. Suetonius *Lives of the Twelve Caesars: Julius* 44. See also Francesca Longo Auricchio, *CErc* 17 (1987) 165.

79. There are, however, scholars so bereft of any sense of humor that they have emended the text to read "I have two libraries—one Greek and one Latin." Better math, granted, but boring; Trimalchio would never boast of being simply as good as anybody else. See R. J. Starr, "Trimalchio's Libraries," *Hermes* 115 (1987) 252f. Trimalchio (whose own name improbably means "thrice king," from Semitic *melech*) would have wanted to seem superior to such Roman book collectors as the grammarian Epaphroditos, who had thirty thousand volumes, and the poet Serenus Sammonicus who had sixty-two thousand.

80. Plotius's name has been plausibly restored in this Paris papyrus to fill out an addressee …]*tie; Hora]tie*, the vocative form of Horace, has also been suggested. See Marcello Gigante, "Plozio non Orazio," *CErc* 3 (1973) 86–87, reprinted in his *Atakta* (Naples, 1993) 167–71.

81. It may be that Siron's name should be spelled Seiron, as both forms are found in Greek inscriptions. The shorter form is found in *PHerc.* 312 (quoted just below), but mistakes in the papyri from *ei* to *i* and (less often) vice versa are common. See Wilhelm Crönert, *Kolotes und Menedemos* (1906; repr., Amsterdam, 1965) 125, n. 532.

82. It has to be noted that many Vergilians do not consider any of the *Catalepton* poems genuine. Neither side in the debate can offer any proof that would convince the other. (A scholar on one side called those on the other "obstinate.") What is undeniable, though, is Vergil's stay in Naples and his early Epicurean leanings. In general, see Marcello Gigante, "Virgilio fra Ercolano e Pompei," in *Virgilio e la Campania* (Naples, 1984) 67–92; Régine Chambert, "Vergil's Epicureanism in His Early Poems," in David Armstrong et al., eds., *Vergil, Philodemus, and the Augustans* (Austin, TX, 2004). For Epicurean themes in Vergil's later (and indisputably authentic) poems the *Eclogues* and *Georgics,* see, respectively, the essays by Gregson Davis and W. R. Johnson in the same volume, pp. 63–74 and 75–83. And on the importance of the (safe) harbor as an Epicurean metaphor, see Francesca Longo Auricchio's essay, again in Armstrong et al., pp. 37–42. See also p. 98.

83. My brief summary of *Ars Poetica* 438–52.

84. F. G. Kenyon, ed., *Aristotle on the Constitution of Athens* (London, 1891—and with two more printings by 1892). A few years later Kenyon was able to publish an even lengthier text when some additional columns were found in Berlin. For a trans., see vol. 20 of the Loeb Classical Library edn. of Aristotle.

85. The Derveni papyrus was burnt when, for reasons that can only be guessed at, it was placed alongside a corpse about to be cremated. For trans. based on the unofficial texts, see André Laks and Glenn W. Most, eds., *Studies on the Derveni Papyrus* (Oxford, 1997) 9–22; and Richard Janko, *Classical Philology* 96 (2001) 1–32. For a bibl. survey of work done on the papyrus up to this point, see Maria Serena Funghi, in Laks and Most, 25–37. Janko has also daringly prepared an "interim" Greek text without having seen the original, but only on the basis of all that has been revealed piecemeal over the years: *ZPE* 141 (2002) 1–62. The most complete discussion is by Gábor Betegh, *The Derveni Papyrus: Cosmology, Theology and Interpretation* (Cambridge, 2004).

86. Another collection of Greek texts saved on papyrus was discovered in Petra, Jordan. See Ludwig Koenen, "Phoenix from the Ashes: The Burnt Archive from Petra," *Michigan Quarterly Review* 35 (1996) 513–31; idem, "The Carbonized Papyri from Petra," *Journal of Roman Archaeology* 86 (1996) 177–88.

87. This was the first location of the Officina dei Papiri. In 1806 it moved to the Palazzo degli Studi (now the

National Archaeological Museum in Naples), where the statues, paintings, vases, etc., excavated from the ruins of Pompeii, Stabiae, and Herculaneum are still housed. In 1927, the Officina and its papyri moved to their current location in the National Library, a part of the Palazzo Reale di Napoli.

88. Quoted from p. 51 of John Hayter, *A Report upon the Herculaneum Manuscripts in a Second Letter, addressed, by permission, to his royal highness the Prince Regent* (London, 1811), which also reprints a second edn. of his first letter (1810). For more on Hayter, see pp. 54f.

89. For a gathering of contemporary texts on the opening of the papyri, see Agnese Travaglione, "Testimonianze su Padre Piaggio," in *Epicuro e l'epicureismo nei papiri ercolanesi* (Naples, 1993) 53–80.

90. Here and in what follows it will be useful to record the Italian words, which are still employed by modern scholars, whatever language they write in. The story of the unrolling of the Herculaneum papyri has been told many times, one particularly clear account being Richard Janko, "*Philodemus resartus*: Progress in Reconstructing the Philosophical Papyri from Herculaneum," *Proceedings of the Boston Area Colloquium in Ancient Philosophy* 7 (1991) 271–308. More detailed and up to date is Blank, "Reflections on Re-reading Piaggio" (see n. 31). Janko goes over the same ground in more detail in his edition of *Philodemus* On Poems, *Book 1* (see n. 6) 15–26 (with more attention paid to the specific text he is editing).

91. *Scorzatura* was at times used to describe the peeling away of layers from the outside of the roll toward the inside, the reverse of what is described above.

92. Personal communication, letter 14 March 2004.

93. For the problems as they pertain to Philodemos's *Rhetoric*, see David Blank, "Matching Tops and Bottoms," in Alexander Jones, ed., *Reconstructing Ancient Texts* (Toronto, 2005).

94. Published in the London *Philosophical Transactions* of 1755 (and reprinted in Comparetti and De Petra [see n. 27] 245f.). For more on Piaggio's machine (the first of several), see Capasso, *Manuale* (see n. 1) 94–98.

95. This is puzzling, as Herculaneum papyri cannot be placed between glass (see below). Perhaps this is a misunderstood reference to the magnifying glasses that were employed to discern, first, whether the unrolling process had unpeeled not one but two layers of papyri, and then to read the obscure letters; see Hayter (see n. 88) 63.

96. Piaggio's account of what Paderni said to him; trans. David Blank.

97. Interestingly, we know numbers three and four in this series in part thanks to the great German art historian Johann Joachim Winckelmann ("Antiquarian to the Pope"), whose 1762 account written in the form of a

letter to Heinrich, Reichsgraf von Brühl, is still worth reading, if not in the original then in the English trans. (of the French trans.): *Critical Account* (see n. 26); the passage describing the unrolling of the first four rolls is on pp. 101f. See further Francesca Longo Auricchio, "Gli scritti ercolanesi di Winckelmann," *CErc* 13 (1983) 179–80; and Blank, "Reflections on Re-reading Piaggio" (see n. 31) 71–78, who details the initial attempts to identify the first papyri to be unrolled.

98. For Obbink's account of how he established the order of frr. of *On Piety* for his 1986 Stanford diss., see his *Philodemus* On Piety (see n. 52) 37–53, esp. 45–50. Delattre's account and edition are in *CErc* 19 (1989) 49–143. See FIG. 76.

99. Lord Nelson was actively engaged in warfare with Napoleon's forces throughout this entire period, much of the time in the Mediterranean, where he often gave support to the kingdom of Naples, indeed sometimes to an extent greater than that desired by the English crown, led as he was by his infatuation with Queen Maria Carolina (and with the wife of the British ambassador to Naples, Emma Hamilton, who may have been encouraged in this affair by the queen).

100. Much of the literature on Hayter is in Italian, but the most interesting document is his own *Second Letter* (see n. 88). See also Francesca Longo Auricchio, "John Hayter nella Officina dei Papiri Ercolanesi," in *Contributi alla storia della Officina dei Papiri Ercolanesi* (see n. 30) 159–215 (which includes an annotated Italian trans. of the *Second Letter*); Giovanni Indelli, "John Hayter e i Papiri Ercolanesi," ibid. 217–25; Walter Scott, *Fragmenta Herculanensia: A Descriptive Catalogue of the Oxford Copies of the Herculanean Rolls* (Oxford, 1885) 2–5; M. J. Mercer, "Hayter, John (1755–1818)," *Oxford Dictionary of National Biography* (Oxford, 2004) 26: 743.

101. Similarly, the massive project of encoding all of Greek literature from Homer until the sixth century A.D. for the CD put out by the *Thesaurus Linguae Graecae* was entrusted to people who were unfamiliar with any Western alphabet. The initial error rate is said to have been remarkably low.

102. For an account of the *disegni*, see Richard Janko and David Blank, "Two New Manuscript Sources for the Texts of the Herculaneum Papyri," *CErc* 28 (1998) 173–84, who recount how Janko, asking for a box of archival material by the wrong number, was surprised to find previously unknown transcriptions made by the people who supervised the *disegnatori*.

103. Napoleon, hardly unique in placing his kin in positions of power, was quoted as saying, "Those who will not rise with me shall no longer be of my family. I am making a family of kings attached to my federal system."

104. See William Drummond and Robert Walpole,

Herculanensia (London, 1810); and Francesca Longo Auricchio, "Sui disegni oxoniensi dei papiri ercolanesi," *CErc* 22 (1992) 181–84. (Later Drummond wrote a best-selling biblical allegory entitled *Oedipus Judaicus*.)

105. The papyri in Britain are now in the Bodleian Library in Oxford and in the British Library in London. See Carlo Knight, "Canguri [kangaroos] e papiri," *CErc* 32 (2002) 305–20.

106. Young described his experiments in the *Quarterly Review* 3 (1810) 18–20.

107. An interesting pamphlet published at this time is *Herculaneum Rolls: Correspondance relative to a proposition by Dr. Sickler of Hildburghausen, upon the subject of their development* (London, 1817), which contains letters in which Thomas Tyrwhitt and Friedrich Sickler try to agree to terms under which the latter would attempt to unroll the papyri, to which he would apply some unspecified liquid that would soften them and so allow for speedier unrolling with a Piaggo-like machine.

108. See Anton Fackelmann, "The Restoration of the Herculaneum Papyri and Other Recent Finds," *Bulletin of the Institute of Classical Studies* 17 (1970) 144–47. Also of great interest is Anna Angeli, "La svolgimento dei papiri carbonizzati," in Capasso, ed., *Il rotolo librario* (see n. 50) 37–104.

109. See Knut Kleve, Espen S. Ore, and Ragnar Jensen, "Letteralogia: Computer e fotografia," *CErc* 17 (1987) 141–50.

110. See Steven W. Booras and D. R. Seely, "Multispectral Imaging of the Herculaneum Papyri," *CErc* 29 (1999) 95–100; Roger T. Macfarlane, "New Readings toward Electronic Publication of *PHerc*. 1084," *CErc* 33 (2003) 16–67. For its use in art, see Mary Miller, "Imaging Maya Art," *Archaeology* 50.3 (1997) 34–40. Multispectral imaging is also used by oncologists to detect melanomas invisible to the naked eye.

111. On palimpsests, see n. 41. With modern techniques now far surpassing all earlier attempts to read palimpsests, an international effort has begun to submit all palimpsests to new computer readings. See Dieter Harlfinger, ed., *Rinascimento virtuale. Digitale Palimpsestforschung. Rediscovering Written Records of a Hidden European Cultural Heritage* (Bratislava, 2002), the proceedings of a conference called to initiate the program. Ultraviolet light, which can make the iron-based ink of medieval mss. fluoresce, is ineffective on the carbon ink of the papyri.

112. See the technical note by Duilio Bertani introducing the images in the *editio princeps* of Poseidippos: Guido Bastianini and Claudio Gallazzi, *Posidippo di Pella: Epigrammi* (*P.Mil.Vogl.* VIII 309) (Milan, 2001). I am also grateful to Prof. Bastianini for showing me the papyrus and the computers and cameras used, as well as explain-

ing the photographic techniques. He is not to be held responsible for any errors on my part.

113. Ancient testimonia on Philodemos are collected in Sider, *Epigrams of Philodemos* (see n. 14) 227–34, the most important of which is Cicero's lengthy description of the friendship between Piso and Philodemos (Cicero *In Pisonem* 68–72 = Testimonium 2 Sider). Cicero, however, alludes to Philodemos anonymously; Horace, most famously, names him in his heavily Epicurean *Satire* 1.2 (= Testimonium 4 Sider, to which should have been added the ancient commentary on this passage ascribed to Acro: "Philodemos was a philosopher of nature, who said that Galli [i.e., castrati] pay a lot to women [as suggested by Horace's poem], either because they are rich or because they are more prone to sexual pleasures. Others say that he [sc. Philodemos] was an Epicurean, who, since he wrote a lot about people of this sort, speaking on the subject of the woman who is difficult [sc. to sleep with], said: 'she should be given to Gallic priests devoted to the Mother of the Gods, since they are unable to lie with women'").

114. Comparetti and De Petra, *La Villa ercolanese* (see n. 27) 79. Their harsh words are repeated and endorsed by Waldstein and Shoobridge, *Herculaneum, Past, Present, and Future* (see n. 25) 83.

115. Thanks to the letter Pliny the Younger wrote about his uncle, we know that Pliny the Elder wrote *The German Wars* in twenty books, a *Life of Pomponius Secundus* in two, and a continuation of a historical work of Aufidius Bassus, in addition to works such as his 38-volume *Natural History*, on other topics.

116. Written in 1819. A "Theban fragment" would be poetry by Pindar. Wishing for lost texts is a game that classicists play in idle moments. My own desiderata would include complete texts of the pre-Socratics Parmenides, Anaxagoras, Herakleitos, and Empedokles. Sometimes, one's wishes are granted: G. della Valle, *Tito Lucrezio Caro e l'epicureismo campano* (Naples, 1933) 216, wished that someday some Lucretius would be found in the Villa dei Papiri, as indeed it has been (see below).

117. Francesca Longo Auricchio and Mario Capasso, "I rotoli della Villa ercolanese: Dislocazione e ritrovamento," *CErc* 17 (1987) 37–47; Capasso, *Manuale* (see n. 1) 65–83.

118. See Daniel Delattre, "Les Mentions de titres d'œuvres dans les livres de Philodème," *CErc* 26 (1996) 143–68.

119. Prepared under the direction of Marcello Gigante (Naples, 1979). The bibliographies have been supplemented by Mario Capasso, "Primo supplemento al *Catalogo dei Papiri Ercolanesi*," *CErc* 19 (1989) 193–264, and Gianluca del Mastro, "Secondo supplemento al *Catalogo dei Papiri Ercolanesi*," *CErc* 30 (2000) 157–241.

120. This term has been subdivided into two stages, preclassical capital and classical capital, both of which are pre-

ceded by early roman; see Knut Kleve, "An Approach to the Latin Papyri from Herculaneum," in *Storia poesia e pensiero nel mondo antico: Studi in onore di Marcello Gigante* (Naples, 1994) 313–20. The majority of the Latin papyri have been dated in the first century B.C. by Paolo Radicotti, "Papiri latini di Ercolano," *Scrittura e Civiltà* 22 (1998) 353–70, at 364. For the rustic capital in its broader context, see also Stanley Morrison, *Politics and Script: Aspects of Authority and Freedom in the Development of Graeco-Latin Script from the Sixth Century B.C. to the Twentieth Century A.D.* (Oxford, 1972) 41–43.

121. See W. M. Lindsay, "The Bodleian Facsimiles of Latin Papyri from Herculaneum," *Classical Review* 4 (1890) 441–45.

122. Hayter has been followed by Marcello Gigante, "Sono di Vario i resti del così detto *Bellum Actiacum* (PHerc. 817)?" in idem, *Altre ricerche filodemee* (Naples, 1998) 87–93.

123. I follow the text of Edward Courtney, *The Fragmentary Latin Poets* (Oxford, 1993) 334–40, who provides a commentary on the Latin text and favors Cornelius Severus as author. For a trans. of all eight columns, see Herbert W. Benario, "The *Carmen de Bello Actiaco* and Early Imperial Epic," *Aufstieg und Niedergang der Römischen Welt* 2.30.3 (1983) 1656–62. Square brackets in the Latin indicate restorations by later scholars of lacunae in the papyrus. I have added (i) the midline dot (· , interpunct) that separates some words, (ii) the distinction sign (/) that marks the end of some lines, (iii) the supraliteral mark, like an acute accent (´), used to note the ictus (beat) or, in one case, a long syllable (*artís* for *artes*), and (iv) the coronis (>–) that marks a new sentence. Commas and periods are modern editorial additions.

124. Knut Kleve, "Lucretius in Herculaneum," *CErc* 19 (1989) 5–27; idem "Lucretius and Philodemus," in K. A. Algra, M. H. Koenen, and P. H. Schrijvers, eds., *Lucretius and His Intellectual Background* (Amsterdam, 1997) 49–66; see also W. Suerbaum, "Herculanensische Lukrez-Papyri," *ZPE* 104 (1994) 1–21. This script has what later were called "small," or lowercase, letters, which, prior to the discovery of these Latin papyri, were thought not to have developed until the fifth century.

125. For what it is worth, my own Lucretius volumes are shelved with my other Latin texts, between Lucan and Manilius, and not with my Epikouros and Philodemos books.

126. In other words, Kleve seems to have guessed and/or hoped that it was Lucretius, and then found that he was right. Somewhat skeptical, I wondered whether these few letters deciphered might not occur in other authors. After a quick search on the Packard Humanities Institute Latin CD—which, although not yet complete for classi-

cal Latin, still contains the bulk of it—I found that the only "hits" were indeed these very passages of Lucretius. Cementing the identification further is the fact that within the three rolls (for books 1, 3, and 5) the relative position of the pieces are known, so that not only does every scrap accord with Lucretius but the identifications come in the right order and at the right locations in Lucretius's text.

127. The manuscripts can be consulted in two excellent facsimiles: Lucretius, *Codex Vossianus Oblongus Phototypice Editus* and *Codex Vossianus Quadratus Phototypice Editus,* ed. Emile Chatelain (Leiden, 1908, 1913).

128. We speak of a "literary fragment" when, typically, one author in a work with a continuous manuscript transmission quotes from a work that is otherwise lost. Thus, anybody claiming to quote from Shakespeare's *Queen Alexandra and Murray* would be giving us a literary fr. of a lost play (if such a play in fact ever existed). What we have with Ennius are literal frr. (scrappy pieces of papyrus) overlapping with literary ones. And see below, where a papyrus of Philodemos provides us with a fr. of Epikouros.

129. The immortality and reincarnation of the soul were denied at great length by Epikouros and Lucretius, but they were an important part of the Greek poet Empedokles' fifth-century didactic epic, which served as a poetic model for Lucretius.

130. E.g., line 104, for its over-the-top alliteration: *O Tite tute Tati tibi tanta tyranne tulisti,* "Thyself to thyself, Titus Tatius the tyrant, thou tookest those terrible troubles" (trans. Warmington). Ennius was also fond of inventing sesquipedalian words on the Homeric model like *sapientipotentes,* "powerfully wise." English trans. of his frr. can be found in E. H. Warmington's *Remains of Old Latin* in the Loeb Classical Library, which also contains the frr. of Caecilius, of whom frr. have likewise been found in Herculaneum (see below). For a more scholarly edition of the *Annales,* see O. Skutsch, *The Annals of Q. Ennius* (Oxford, 1985), whose line numbers I cite.

131. (i) On line 184 the papyrus reading *non* agrees with ms. *p* of Cicero against the *nec* of the others; and (ii) on line 189 the papyrus agrees with the medieval manuscripts in reading *eorundem me libertati parcere certum est,* against the conjecture of the famous textual critic Lachmann, who argued for transposing *me* and *libertati.* See Knut Kleve, "Ennius in Herculaneum," *CErc* 20 (1990) 5–16; idem, "Phoenix from the Ashes: Lucretius and Ennius in Herculaneum," *The Norwegian Institute at Athens* (1991) 57–64. Thus, unlike Diels, Lachmann has not been vindicated by papyrus reading discovered after his death. He may still be right—Skutch was tempted to print his transposition in his edition of the *Annals*—since no text, however early, is free of error, but it remains a conjecture.

The basic metrics of the line remain unchanged with the transposition (that is, all spondees except for the fifth foot in both cases), but as the papyrus and the mss. have it, there is no midline caesura (word break) in either of the expected places, a metrical shape Ennius allows only rarely (0.8%). The transposition provides the missing caesura (*libertati | me*).

132. Dots under letters mark those incomplete but reasonably certain. The raised dot (interpunct) is used to mark the division between words, although some common combinations were not so marked; for example, *neque hilo,* "nor any," with which compare *nihil,* which is the same pairing of the negative *ne* and *hilum,* "not one bit" (the *-que* is a postpositive "and").

133. The first notice in print of the contents of this roll was by Knut Kleve, "How to Read an Illegible Papyrus: Towards an Edition of *PHerc.* 78, Caecilius Statius, *Obolostates sive Faenerator,*" *CErc* 26 (1996) 5–14.

134. For his previously known frr., along with English trans., see the first vol. of Warmington's *Remains of Old Latin* (see n. 130), which also includes all the frr. of Ennius.

135. Old Comedy (extant complete only in Aristophanes) contains plots involving politics and/or literary references that cannot be divorced from the accompanying vulgarity; New Comedy, depending almost entirely on domestic squabbles and misunderstandings, is less intellectually demanding and has therefore historically been more successful. It also translates from one culture to another far more easily than Aristophanes. Consider the chain linking a lost play of Menander to Plautus's *Menaechmi* to Shakespeare's *A Comedy of Errors* to Rodgers and Hart's *The Boys from Syracuse.*

136. What little can be discerned in these scrappy papyri is discussed by the great Latin palaeographer W. M. Lindsay (see n. 121).

137. Kleve, "An Approach to the Latin Papyri" (see n. 120) 319.

138. *PHerc.* 862 and 1485 are two copies of the same text; see Mario Capasso, "Un libro filodemeo in due esemplari," *CErc* 18 (1998) 139–48. Among other texts, there are duplicate copies of Philodemos's *Rhetoric, Poems,* and *Pragmateiai.* See below, on *PHerc.* 1021 and 164.

139. For a summary of Philodemos's life, schooling, and travels, see Sider, *Epigrams of Philodemos* (see n. 14) 3–24. Between Athens and Italy, Philodemos may have spent time in Rhodes (where there was a thriving Epicurean community), Alexandria, and the Sicilian town of Himera. Arguing for an Alexandrian stay is E. Puglia, "Filodemo da Alessandria ad Atene," in Mario Capasso, ed., *Da Ercolano all'Egitto* (Galatina, 1999) 133–42. On Gadara, see John T. Fitzgerald, "Gadara: Philodemus' Native City," in John T. Fitzgerald, Dirk Obbink, and Glenn S. Holland, eds., *Philodemus and the New Testament World* (Leiden, 2004) 343–97.

140. Guglielmo Cavallo, *Libri scritture scribi a Ercolano: Introduzione allo studio dei materiali greci.* Primo supplemento a *CErc* 13 (1983). For more on the handwriting of the papyri of *On Nature,* see Janko, "The Herculaneum Library" (see n. 44) 39f.

141. Much of the work on these new texts of Epikouros *On Nature* has been done by Giuliana Leone, David Sedley, and Simon Laursen, all published in *CErc.* Some have been collected (with Italian trans.) in Graziano Arrighetti, *Epicuro,* 2nd edn. (Turin, 1973), 186–379, but it will be many years before a comprehensive edition of all known passages will be attempted. English trans. of a very few of the new Epikouros texts may be found in A. A. Long and David N. Sedley, *The Hellenistic Philosophers* (Cambridge, 1987) 1.99, 102–4; 2.113; and in Brad Inwood, L. P. Gerson, and D. S. Hutchinson, *The Epicurus Reader: Selected Writings and Testimonia* (Indianapolis, 1994) 76–77. Other books of *On Nature* will be prepared by Leone and Annamaria D'Angelo.

142. The most complete collection from literary sources of testimony and quotation from *On Nature* can be found in Hermann Usener's still-useful collection of texts, *Epicurea* (Leipzig, 1887) 124–30.

143. David Sedley, "The Structure of Epicurus' *On Nature,*" *CErc* 4 (1974) 89–92 (here I am quoting from p. 89), building on his earlier article "Epicurus, *On Nature,* Book XXVIII," *CErc* 3 (1973) 5–83. On the subject of this work's organization, see also Graziano Arrighetti, "L'Opera *Sulla natura* di Epicuro," *CErc* 1 (1971) 41–56.

144. See Knut Kleve and Gianluca del Mastro, "Il *PHerc.* 1533: Zenone Sidonio *A Cratero,*" *CErc* 30 (2000) 149–56. We do not know who this Krateros is.

145. For an extensive list of the works Philodemos mentions, see Delattre, "Les Mentions de titres" (see n. 118). Most, of course, are to philosophical works, and of these most are to Epicureans (including himself), but he makes frequent, albeit hostile, references, also to ten Stoics and four Cynics, as well as to Demokritos, Plato (and Academics), and Aristotle (and Peripatetics).

146. Thus, in a papyrus letter written in the mid-first century A.D., someone tells his friend that he will send Epicurean books by Metrodoros and Epikouros, but does not mention Philodemos. See J. G. Keenan, "A Papyrus Letter about Epicurean Philosophy," *The J. Paul Getty Museum Journal* 5 (1977) 91–94.

147. None of Philodemos's epigrams has been found in the Villa, even though they were published and widely read and admired, as Cicero explicitly tells us. In time, they were anthologized by Philip of Thessalonika, probably at the end of the first century A.D., and eventually some portion of them made their way into a more compendious Byzantine collection known now as the *Greek Anthology,* which includes later anthologies as well. See

109

Alan Cameron, *The Greek Anthology from Meleager to Planudes* (Oxford, 1993). All that is left on papyri of Philodemos's epigrams is a list of *incipits* (i.e., only the first word or first few words), now housed in the Sackler Library in Oxford, many of which overlap with previously known epigrams of Philodemos. For more on this *incipit* list, see Sider, *Epigrams of Philodemos* (see n. 14) 203–5; and Francesca Maltomini, "Considerazioni su *P.Oxy.* LIV 3724: Struttura e finalità di una lista di incipit epigrammatistici," *ZPE* 144 (2003) 67–75.

This account of Philodemos's treatises, although looking at them in the first instance as physical objects, owes much to the vast literature on their philosophical contents, *in primis* the broad overviews in Robert Phillipson, "Philodemos," *Paulys Realencyclopädie der classischen Altertumswissenschaft* (Stuttgart, 1938) 19: 2444–82; Elizabeth Asmis, "Philodemus' Epicureanism," in Wolfgang Haase and Hildegard Temporini, eds., *Aufstieg und Niedergang der Römischen Welt* 2.36.4 (Berlin, 1990) 2369–2406; Tiziano Dorandi, "Filodemo: Gli orientamenti della ricerca attuale," ibid. 2328–68; Gigante, *Philodemus in Italy* (see n. 14).

148. Diogenes Laertios 10.3. Diogenes is probably drawing on this same work of Philodemos later (10.24) when he says that, according to Philodemos, Epikouros's successor Polyainos was "just and amiable." On Philodemos's historical writings, see Tiziano Dorandi, "Filodemo storico del pensiero antico," in Haase and Temporini, *Aufstieg und Niedergang* (see n. 147) 2407–23; Giovanni Arrighetti, "Filodemo biografo dei filosofi e le forme dell'erudizione," *CErc* 33 (2003) 13–30.

149. See Jørgen Mejer, *Diogenes Laertius and His Hellenistic Background* (Wiesbaden, 1978) 69–74; Marcello Gigante, "Biografia e dossografia in Diogene Laerzio," *Elenchos* 7 (1986) 25–34.

150. Edited twice in recent years: (i) Konrad Gaiser, *Philodems Akademica: Die Bericht über Platon und die Alte Akademie in zwei herkulanensischen Papyri* (Stuttgart, 1988), with German trans.; Gaiser, however, edited only the columns dealing directly with Plato (the Old Academy of the subtitle). For the complete Greek text, see (ii) Tiziano Dorandi, *Filodemo: Storia dei Filosofi: Platone e l'Academia* (Naples, 1991), with Italian trans. For an account of its contents (in the form of a review of Gaiser), see Jonathan Barnes, "Philodemus and the Old Academy," *Apeiron* 22 (1989) 139–48.

151. For this question in general, see Giovanni Indelli, "Platone in Filodemo," *CErc* 16 (1986) 109–12. Socrates too could not be dismissed outright by Epicureans; see Knut Kleve, "Scurra Atticus: The Epicurean View of Socrates," in Συζήτησις: *Studi sull'epicurismo greco e romano offerti a Marcello Gigante* (Naples, 1983) 227–51.

152. It has been edited with an introduction and commen-
tary by Tiziano Dorandi, *Storia dei filosofi: La stoà da Zenone a Panezio* (PHerc. *1018*) (Leiden, 1994).

153. The text has been prepared by Tiziano Dorandi, "Filodemo, Gli Stoici (*P.Herc.* 155 e 339)," *CErc* 12 (1982) 91–133.

154. For a brief overview of what is known of Zenon's *Republic*, see Malcolm Schofield, in Keimpe Algra et al., eds., *The Cambridge History of Hellenistic Philosophy* (Cambridge, 1999) 756–60; more detail in Malcolm Schofield, *The Stoic Idea of the City* (Chicago, 1999), passim.

155. Anna Angeli, *Filodemo: Agli amici di scuola* (PHerc. *1005*) (Naples, 1988).

156. The work has been edited by Adele Tepedino Guerra, "L'Opera filodemea *Su Epicuro* (PHerc. 1232, 1289 β)," *CErc* 24 (1994) 5–53.

157. This work has been edited by Cesira Militello, *Memorie Epicuree* (PHerc. *1418 e 310*) (Naples, 1997).

158. See Diskin Clay, "The Cults of Epicurus," in idem, *Paradosis and Survival: Three Chapters in the Epicurean Philosophy* (Ann Arbor, 1998) 75–102, who gathers and trans. all the ancient testimony on this practice.

159. That is, tales more entertaining than those Odysseus narrated to the Phaeacians in the *Odyssey*, Books 9–12, such as his adventures with the Kyklops, Kirke, and the man-eating Lestrygonians.

160. Hence the two lasting pejorative uses of his name: In English as well as other languages an Epicurean is someone devoted, perhaps overly so, to fancy food and wine; in Hebrew and Yiddish an *apikoiros* is a free thinker if not an outright atheist. On the other hand, early Christianity found much to admire and emulate in Epicurean ideas of community and friendship; see Clarence E. Glad, *Paul and Philodemus: Adaptability in Epicurean and Early Christian Psychagogy* (Leiden, 1995). See also three essays in *Philodemus and the New Testament World* (see n. 139): Benjamin Fiore, "The Pastoral Epistles in the Light of Philodemus's *On Frank Criticism*" (271–93); J. Paul Sampley, "Paul's Frank Speech with the Galatians and the Corinthians" (295–321); and Bruce W. Winter, "Philodemus and Paul on Rhetorical Delivery" (323–42).

161. Another example of confusion on the title page occurred when Winckelmann identified a work as that of Phanias, a common enough Greek name. On further examination, however, this was discovered to be a work by Philodemos, *On Arrogance* (*Peri Hyperphanias*), ed. Christian Jensen (Leipzig, 1911); cf. p. 88 here.

162. The most complete edition, with German commentary, of the Greek text of Book 1 and (as he calls it) Book 3 is by Hermann Diels, *Philodemos über die Götter. Erstes und drittes Buch* (1916–1917; repr. Leipzig, 1970); an earlier text, with English commentary, of both books can be found in Scott, *Fragmenta Herculanensia* (see n. 100)

93–152. Book 3 has been partially reedited by Graziano Arrighetti, *Parola del Passato* 44 (1955) 322–56, and idem, *Studi Classici e Orientali* 7 (1958) 83–99. Knut Kleve is preparing a new edition and commentary. See Knut Kleve, "The Unknown Parts of Philodemus, *On the Gods,* Book One, *PHerc.* 26," *Elenchos* 25 (1996) 671–81. Kleve and P. Tidemandsen are preparing a new edition of Book 1; Mariacarolina Santoro is working on Book 3.

163. The symbol //, devised by *On Piety*'s editor, Dirk Obbink, indicates that "the fragments of these two series alternate and link vertically"; that is, as the columns originally wrapped around the roll, they passed from what is now *PHerc.* 1787 to 1098 and back again (see FIG. 76). All that I have simplified here is explained in impressive detail by Obbink, *Philodemus* On Piety (see n. 52), with trans. and commentary.

164. For an account of Epikouros's theory of the gods and his attitude toward religion, see, in addition to Obbink's introduction to Part 1 of *On Piety* (see n. 52) 1–23, John Rist, *Epicurus: An Introduction* (Cambridge, 1972) 140–63.

165. Phillip Howard De Lacy and Estelle Allen De Lacy, *Philodemos. On Methods of Inference,* 2nd edn. (Naples, 1978). The supplementary essays in this volume are particularly helpful.

166. For a learned and entertaining account of what the Greeks made of the many dinosaur bones they found, see Adrienne Mayor, *The First Fossil Hunters: Paleontology in Greek and Roman Times* (Princeton, 2000).

167. *Oikonomia* is the Greek word for this, but its English descendant "economy" has far wider import. The old-fashioned term "home economics" returns to the original notion.

168. On this last point, it has been noticed that Vergil incorporated Epicurean notions of appropriate rage into his characterization of Aeneas. See Giovanni Indelli, "Filodemo e Virgilio sull'ira (*PHerc.* 495 e 558)," *CErc* 31 (2001) 31–36; Michael Erler, "Der Zorn des Helden: Philodems *De Ira* und Vergils Konzept des Zorns in der *Aeneis*," *Grazer Beiträge* 18 (1992) 103–26. And for Vergil's relationship with Philodemos in general, see Armstrong et al., eds., *Vergil, Philodemus, and the Augustans* (see n. 82).

169. On the Democritean background, see James Warren, *Epicurus and Democritean Ethics: An Archaeology of* Ataraxia (Cambridge, 2002). *Ataraxia* is that desirable state of being in which we are not disturbed by the world around us. (From this Greek word derives the trade name for the tranquilizer Atarax, which is designed to accomplish through chemical means what Epikouros trained his followers to achieve on their own.)

170. For English trans. of this work, see Appendix 2. See also Marcello Gigante, "Filodemo sulla libertà di parola," in

idem, *Ricerche filodemee,* 2nd edn. (Naples, 1983) 55–113.

171. The column numbers in this work have *a* and *b* attached to them because this papyrus roll was one of those broken into top and bottom, with, of course, some loss between them. The top half is thus (for example) 24a, the bottom half, assuming that the two separate halves have been properly correlated, is 24b. There are also many isolated frr., whose place in the run of columns cannot be determined. See Blank, "Matching Tops and Bottoms" (see n. 93).

172. Thus, as noted earlier (p. 7), in his *Ars Poetica,* which owes much to Philodemos's treatises on poetic theory (see next section), Horace praises Quintilius because he will not flatter a friend's (i.e., Horace's) poetry, but rather will offer only honest criticism (438–52); that is, Horace imports Epicurean ideas of *parrhesia* into literary criticism.

173. Trans. Sandra Sider.

174. The other three, as given by Philodemos, are "the gods cause no fear," "the Good is obtainable," and "the Bad is endurable." On the *tetrapharmakos,* see Dirk Obbink, "Philodemus' *De Pietate:* Argument, Organization, and Authorship," *Atti del v. Seminario Internazionale di Papirologia. Lecce 27–29 giugno 1994,* ed. Mario Capasso (Galatina, 1994) 218–20, who shows how recitation to oneself of these four lines in a semiritualistic fashion could soften one's pain.

175. The only complete edition, with Dutch trans. and commentary, is Taco Kuiper, *Philodemus over den dood* (Amsterdam, 1925). The first nine columns and the last three (cols. 37–39) were reedited, with Italian trans. and commentary, by Gigante, *Ricerche filodemee* (see n. 170) 115–234. It is unfortunate that Gigante was unable to finish his planned complete edition of this text before his death. An Italian trans. was prepared by Ruggero Sammartano, *Filodemo di Gadara: I Frammenti del iv libro dell'opera "Sulla Morte"* (Rome, 1970). The work will be edited by Francesca Longo Auricchio.

176. See in particular Elizabeth Asmis, "Epicurean Poetics," in Dirk Obbink, ed., *Philodemus and Poetry: Poetic Theory and Practice in Lucretius, Philodemus, and Horace* (New York, 1995) 15–34, followed by my response, 35–41.

177. An excellent collection of ancient Greek and Roman texts on this topic can be found in Donald A. Russell and Michael Winterbottom, *Ancient Literary Criticism: The Principal Texts in New Translations* (Oxford, 1972), from which, however, the fragmentary remains of Philodemos are notably absent. For an overview, see G. M. A. Grube, *The Greek and Roman Critics* (Toronto, 1965), who was one of the first to treat Philodemos's theories in a book of this sort; and Donald A. Russell, *Criticism in Antiquity* (London, 1981). Although still useful, these two books have been overtaken by recent

work on Philodemos, which has revealed much about his immediate predecessors. See now the various essays in Obbink, *Philodemus and Poetry* (see n. 176) and the articles by Elizabeth Asmis: "The Poetic Theory of the Stoic 'Aristo,'" *Apeiron* 23 (1990) 147–201; "Crates on Poetic Criticism," *Phoenix* 46 (1991) 138–69; "Neoptolemus and the Classification of Poetry," *Classical Philology* 87 (1992) 206–31; and "An Epicurean Survey of Poetic Theories (Philodemus *On Poems* 5, cols. 26–36)," *Classical Quarterly* 42 (1992) 395–415. For a briefer overview, see Nicola Pace, "Problematiche di poetica in Filodemo," *CErc* 25 (1995) 111–90.

178. The generous support given by the National Endowment for the Humanities to the Philodemus Translation Project is showing results: Richard Janko's edition of Book 1 of Philodemos's *On Poems* has already been published (see n. 6), and others are scheduled that will cover all the aesthetic works (on poetry, music, and rhetoric). In addition to these works specifically dedicated to the subject, Book 2 of Philodemos's *On Piety* devotes much of its space to the role of the gods in poetry; see Appendix 2.

179. For their views, which will be given here only when they pertain to Philodemos, see the introductions by Richard Janko et al. to their several editions of the books of Philodemos *On Poems* (Oxford, 2002–), and the interesting series of articles by Asmis (see n. 177). For Krates, see Maria Broggiato, *Cratete di Mallo: I frammenti* (La Spezia, 2001).

180. Nicknames were common in Philodemos's circle. Vergil, for example, had his name falsely derived from *virgo*, "young girl," so that he could be called Parthenias, which is the Greek equivalent of *virgo;* furthermore, Parthenias sounded somewhat like Pathenope, the Siren who gave her name to the site that was later called Naples, where Vergil lived (and where he is buried). Note the end of Vergil's *Georgics,* where he provides a "seal," that is, a kind of end-title worked into the text by the author himself: "At that time sweet Parthenope nursed Vergil as he flourished while working in ignoble ease" (4.563–4).

181. Philodemos had nothing but praise for Sappho, both in his epigrams (12 Sider = *Anthologia Palatina* 5.132) and elsewhere in his theoretical writings (most notably in *On Poems* 5, cols. 37.2–38.15 Mangoni); for trans. and discussion, see Sider, *Epigrams of Philodemos* (see n. 14) 28–31.

182. Actually, this Latin tag was invented for Goldwyn by Howard Dietz, who, before he became a well-known lyricist of popular songs ("Dancing in the Dark," "That's Entertainment"), worked for MGM as head of advertising and publicity. See Kenneth Lapatin, "The Fate of Plate and Other Precious Materials: Toward a Histo-

riography of Ancient Greek Minor(?) Arts," in A. A. Donohue and Mark D. Fullerton, eds., *Ancient Art and Its Historiography* (Cambridge, 2003) 88 n. 38, who also notes the French phrase *l'art pour l'art* coined by Benjamin Constant in 1804. Philodemos, it has to be admitted, has nothing this nifty.

183. We learn of this from a thirteenth-century author, Ibn abi Uṣaybiʿa, who had access to the now-lost work of Galen, where he recounts this story. Conceivably in the original, Galen, who tended to be chatty about his own life and books, gave a much more complete list of the books he lost (Ibn abi Uṣaybiʿa, *ʿUyūn al-anbāʾ fi ṭabaḳāt al-aṭibbāʾ,* ed. A. Müller [Cairo, 1882] 1.84.31–85.2). Alpha-betizing books on the shelf or in catalogue lists goes back to Aristotle, who arranged his collection of over   a hundred Greek constitutions alphabetically by city. See Lloyd W. Daly, *Contributions to a History of Alpha-betization in Antiquity and the Middle Ages,* Collection Latomus, 90 (Brussels, 1967).

GLOSSARY

biblos/biblion	Gr. Book roll.
codex/codices	A book bound in the modern format.
coronis	From Gr. *koronis* (crow's beak), a curved, often elaborate marker with the same function as a *paragraphos*.
disegno/disegni	Ital. "Drawing," the exact drawing, or transcription, of all marks on a papyrus roll, made as preparation for publication of the text.
incipit	L. "It begins." First words of a text (used to identify a work when title is missing).
interpunct	Raised dot used to separate words in some L. texts.
kollema/kollemata	Gr. Individual dried sheet of papyrus, which, when joined to other sheets will form a papyrus roll.
kollesis/kolleseis	Gr. Overlap of individual papyrus sheets to form a roll.
lacuna	L. "Gap," as a missing space in a papyrus text.
midollo/midolli	Ital. "Marrow," the center of a papyrus roll.
nuée ardente	French, "burning cloud," a volcanic release of burning hot gases and incandescent rocks.
papyrus	(i) A plant, (ii) a writing surface (paper) made from this plant, (iii) a long roll constructed from separate sheets, and (iv) a text written on this material.
paragraphos	Gr. Straight horizontal line extending a short distance from the margin into a text. Used to mark the end of a text, the beginning of a quotation, or a change from one speaker to another (in drama).
PHerc.	*Papyrus Herculanensis* (pl. *Papyri Herculanenses*). All the papyri found in the Villa dei Papiri are numbered under this rubric. Exceptions are those now in Paris: *P.Herc.Paris*. The rolls sent to England (now in the Bodleian Library in Oxford and in the British Library in London) in addition have call numbers appropriate to their respective libraries, e.g., *PHerc* 118a =*Bodl.Libr.Ms.Gr.Class.C.* 10.
pyroclastic flow	The stream of hot rocks and mud and everything that is dragged along with it during a volcanic eruption.

scorza/scorze	Ital. "Bark" or "husk," the outer layers of a papyrus roll.
scorzatura	Ital. "Husking," the method of peeling off scorched outer layers of a papyrus roll in order to get to the less charred inner part of the roll.
selis/selides	Gr. Column of text on a papyrus roll. L. *pagina/paginae.*
sillybos/sillyboi	Gr. Tag, attached to the top edge of a papyrus roll, on which the contents of the roll were identified, like a spine on a modern book.
sottoposto	Ital. "Placed under," used of a fragment of papyrus that adheres to a part of the papyrus roll later on the roll to which it did not originally belong.
sovraposto	Ital. "Placed above," used of a fragment of papyrus that adheres to an earlier part of the paryrus roll to which it did not originally belong.
subscriptio	L. End-title, or, title of a work written at the end of the text.
umbilicus	L. "Navel," wood dowel attached to the beginning and/or end of a papyrus roll to facilitate its rolling.

Annotated Bibliography

116

Allen, Walter, and Phillip de Lacy. 1939. "The Patrons of Philodemus." *Classical Philology* 34: 59–65.

Armstrong, David, et al., eds. 2004. *Vergil, Philodemus, and the Augustans.* Austin, TX.

Auricchio, Francesca Longo. 1997. "Le prime scoperte a Ercolano." *CErc* 27: 175–79.

Blanck, Horst. 1992. *Das Buch in der Antike.* Munich.

Blank, David. 1989. "Reflections on Re-reading Piaggio and the Early History of the Herculaneum Papyri." *CErc* 29: 55–82.

Bloch, Herbert. 1940. "L. Calpurnius Piso Caesoninus in Samothrace and Herculaneum." *American Journal of Archaeology* 44: 485–93.

Capasso, Mario. 1989. "Primo supplemento al *Catalogo dei Papiri Ercolanesi.*" *CErc* 19: 193–264.

———. 1991. *Manuale di papirologia ercolanese.* Galatina.

———, ed. 1994. *Il rotolo librario: Fabbricazione, restauro, organizzazione interna.* Galatina.

———. 1995. *Volumen: Aspetti della tipologia del rotolo librario antico.* Naples. Discussion of the various parts of the book roll and their Gr. and L. names.

Casson, Lionel. 2001. *Libraries in the Ancient World.* New Haven.

Cavallo, Guglielmo. 1983. *Libri scritture scribi a Ercolano: Introduzione allo studio dei materiali greci.* Primo supplemento a *Cronache Ercolanesi*, 13. A palaeographical study of the Herculaneum papyri designed to distinguish among scribal hands and to establish dates for the writing of the papyri.

Comparetti, Domenico, and Giulio De Petra. 1972. *La Villa ercolanese dei Pisoni: I suoi monumenti e la sua biblioteca.* 1883. Repr. with a note by A. de Franciscis. Naples.

Delattre, Daniel. 1996. "Les Mentions de titres d´œuvres dans les livres de Philodème." *CErc* 26: 143–68.

Del Mastro, Gianluca. 2000. "Secondo supplemento al *Catalogo dei Papiri Ercolanesi.*" *CErc* 30: 157–241.

Dorandi, Tiziano. 1989. "Testimonianze ercolanesi." In *Corpus dei Papiri Filosofici Greci e Latini. Parte 1: Autori Noti*, Vol. 1*: 1–78. Florence. An index of all the philosophers, sophists, and medical authors named in the Herculaneum papyri. (Thus, no mention of poets.)

———. 2000. *Le Style et la tablette dans le secret des auteurs antiques.* Paris.

Fitzgerald, John T., Dirk Obbink, and Glenn S. Holland, eds. 2004. *Philodemus and the New Testament World.* Leiden.

Gigante, Marcello, ed. 1979a. *Catalogo dei papiri ercolanesi.* Naples. Updated by two supplements; see Capasso 1989 and Del Mastro 2000.

———. 1979b. *Civiltà delle forme letterarie nell'antica Pompei.* Naples.

———. 1989. *Il Fungo sul Vesuvio secondo Plinio il Giovane.* Rome.

———. 2002. *Philodemus in Italy: The Books from Herculaneum.* Trans. Dirk Obbink. Ann Arbor. (The 2002 paperback silently corrects errors and updates the bibl. of the 1995 hardback.)

Hayter, John. 1811. *A Report upon the Herculaneum Manuscripts in a Second Letter, addressed, by permission, to his royal highness the Prince Regent.* London.

Immerwahr, Henry R. 1964. "Book Rolls on Attic Vases." In Charles Henderson, Jr., ed. *Classical, Mediaeval, and Renaissance Studies in Honor of Berthold Louis Ullman.* Vol. 1: 17–48. Rome.

———. 1973. "More Book Rolls on Attic Vases." *Antike Kunst* 16: 143–47.

Irigoin, Jean. 2001. *Le Livre grec des origines à la Renaissance.* Paris.

Janko, Richard. 2002. "The Herculaneum Library: Some Recent Developments." *Estudios Clásicos* 121: 25–41.

Jashemski , Wilhelmina Feemster, and Frederick G. Meyer, eds. 2002. *A Natural History of Pompeii.* Cambridge.

Kenyon, Frederic G. 1951. *Book and Readers in Ancient Greece and Rome*. 2nd edn. Oxford.

Legras, Bernard. 2002. *Lire en Égypte d'Alexandre à l'Islam*. Paris.

Lewis, Naphtali. 1974. *Papyrus in Classical Antiquity*. Oxford.

Macfarlane, Roger T. 2003. "New Readings toward Electronic Publication of *PHerc*. 1084." *CErc* 33: 16–67.

Murray, Oswyn. 1965. "Philodemus on the Good King according to Homer." *The Journal of Roman Studies* 55: 161–82.

Obbink, Dirk, ed. 1995. *Philodemus and Poetry: Poetic Theory and Practice in Lucretius, Philodemus, and Horace*. New York.

———. 1997. "Imaging the Carbonized Papyri from Herculaneum." *Literary and Linguistic Computing* 12: 159–61.

Parkinson, Richard, and Stephen Quirke. 1995. *Papyrus*. London.

Parslow, Christopher. 1995. *Rediscovering Antiquity: Karl Weber and the Excavation of Herculaneum, Pompeii, and Stabiae*. Cambridge.

Pfeiffer, Rudolf. 1968. *History of Classical Scholarship, from the Beginning to the End of the Hellenistic Age*. Oxford.

Platthy, Jeno. 1968. *Sources on the Earliest Greek Libraries*. Amsterdam.

Roberts, Colin. 1963. *Buried Books in Antiquity: Habent Sua Fata Libelli*. Arundell Esdaile Memorial Lecture, 1962. London.

——— and T. C. Skeat. 1983. *The Birth of the Codex*. London.

Schubart, Wilhelm. 1962. *Das Buch bei den Griechen und Römern*. 3rd edn. Heidelberg.

Sider, David. 1997. *The Epigrams of Philodemos*. New York.

Skeat, T. C. 1956. "The Use of Dictation in Ancient Book Production." *Proceedings of the British Academy* 42: 179–208.

Tait, Jane I. M. 1941. *Philodemus' Influence on the Latin Poets*. Ph.D. diss., Bryn Mawr College.

Turner, Eric G. 1952. *Athenian Books in the Fifth and Fourth Centuries b.c.* Inaugural Lecture, Univ. College London.

———. 1968. *Greek Papyri: An Introduction*. Oxford.

———. 1971. *Greek Manuscripts of the Ancient World*. Princeton. Chiefly black-and-white photographs of papyri with transcriptions and palaeographical and editorial notes.

———. 1973. *The Papyrologist at Work*. Greek, Roman and Byzantine Monograph 6. Durham, N.C. An introduction to the editing of a papyrus text.

Winckelmann, Johann Joachim. 1771. *Critical Account of the Situation and Destruction by the First Eruptions of Mount Vesuvius of Herculaneum, Pompeii, and Stabia . . .* London.

Wojcik, Maria Rita. 1986. *La Villa dei Papiri ad Ercolano: Contributo alla ricostruzione dell'ideologia della* nobilitas *tardorepubblicana*. Rome.

Index